A VERY GALLANT GENTLEMAN

Colonel Francis Thornhagh (1617–1648) and the Nottinghamshire Horse

Stuart B. Jennings

'This is the Century of the Soldier', Fulvio Testi, Poet, 1641

Helion & Company

Helion & Company Limited
Unit 8 Amherst Business Centre
Budbrooke Road
Warwick
CV34 5WE
England
Tel. 01926 499 619
Email: info@helion.co.uk
Website: www.helion.co.uk
Twitter: @helionbooks
Visit our blog http://blog.helion.co.uk/

Published by Helion & Company 2022
Designed and typeset by Serena Jones
Cover designed by Paul Hewitt, Battlefield Design (www.battlefield-design.co.uk)

Front cover; Colonel Francis Thornhagh, *c.* 1640. Artist Unknown. With thanks to the late G. M. T. Foljambe Esq. of Osberton for use of this image.

ISBN 978-1-915070-34-0

British Library Cataloguing-in-Publication Data.
A catalogue record for this book is available from the British Library.

For details of other military history titles published by Helion & Company Limited, contact the above address, or visit our website: http://www.helion.co.uk

We always welcome receiving book proposals from prospective authors.

Contents

Timeline for the Life of Colonel Francis Thornhagh

National events that were important but did not directly involve Francis Thornhagh are recorded in *Italic*.

Year	Date	Event
1617		Birth of Francis, to Sir Francis and his wife Jane at Fenton
1625	*3 March*	*Death of James I and accession of Charles I*
c. 1625–34		Educated at Lincoln Grammar School
1635	8 May	Matriculated at Magdalen College, Oxford
1636	November	Admitted to Inner Temple
1638		*First Anglo-Scottish Bishops' War*
c. 1638–39		Military service in the Netherlands
1640	*April*	*Short Parliament*
	August	*Second Bishops War*
	November	*Long Parliament*
	Before Advent	Marriage to Elizabeth St Andrews of Gotham
c. 1642		Birth of Francis and Elizabeth's first child
1642		Appointed Magistrate
	22 August	*Charles raises the royal standard at Nottingham, marking the formal start of the Civil War*
	25 October	*Battle of Edgehill between the armies of Charles I and those of Parliament*
	December	Sir Francis Thornhagh receives commission from Parliament to raise a regiment of horse in Nottinghamshire. His son, Francis, to be appointed as Lieutenant Colonel.
1643	28 April	Death of Sir Francis Thornhagh. His son Francis inherits the estate but his widowed mother, Jane, retains the house at Fenton as a dower. Appointed colonel and commander of the regiment his father had raised.

Year	Date	Event
	28 July	Battle of Gainsborough. Fighting alongside Oliver Cromwell, taken prisoner, stripped of his armour and then wounded.
	30 December	Appointed High Sheriff of Nottingham
1644	16 January	3,000 Royalist soldiers surprise the town of Nottingham and make their way up to the foot of the castle. Thornhagh dismounts his cavalry and leads them out of the castle to drive them out of the town by street to street fighting.
	29 February to 21 March	Francis at the second siege of Newark. Leads charge of Nottingham horse against the relief force of Prince Rupert. Seriously wounded by shot to stomach and arm. Carried back to Nottingham in a wagon and out of action for most of the summer.
	2 July	Defeat of Newcastle and Rupert's forces at Marston Moor
	2 August	Thornhagh considered well enough to be appointed governor at recently taken Welbeck House
		Colonel Thornhagh confirmed by commission as commander, second only to Lord Fairfax, of all Parliamentarian horse in Nottinghamshire
	07 December	Thornhagh surprises party of Royalist horse at Muskham Bridge taking both prisoners and colours
	December	At end of month, takes fortified house of local Royalist Sir Roger Cooper at Thurgaton, sending Sir Roger as prisoner to Nottingham
1645	January to June	Thornhagh and Nottingham horse watch and harass the Newark garrison
	14 June	*Royalist army defeated at the Battle of Naseby*
	20 June	Parliamentary Ordinance issued for the creation of a Northern Association army under the command of Colonel General Poyntz. Thornhagh and Nottingham horse incorporated into this field army.
	24 September	Battle of Rowton Heath outside Chester. Thornhagh leads charge that routs the Royalist horse under Lord Charles Gerard, helping Poyntz to win the battle
	3 November	At the storming of Shelford Manor and garrison in Nottinghamshire
1645–46	26 November to 6 May	Third and final siege of Newark. Present over the course of the whole siege and a significant signatory to the surrender document on behalf of Parliament
1646	January/ February	Elected MP for Retford

Year	Date	Event
1647	July	Breach between the Houses of Parliament and the Army. Thornhagh one of the 58 MPs who leave London to place themselves under the protection of Lord Fairfax and the army.
1648	27 January	Baptism of John Thornhagh, son and heir to Francis
	8 May to 11 July	Campaign in Wales and siege of Pembroke Castle by Oliver Cromwell with Thornhagh and Nottingham horse present
	3 August	Cromwell at Nottingham and with Thornhagh and Nottingham horse sets out to confront the Scottish army under the command of the Duke of Hamilton
1648	17–9 August	Defeat of Scottish forces at the battle of Preston
1648	18 August	Colonel Francis Thornhagh killed by Scottish lancers while leading a charge against the fleeing Scots near Chorley
1648	22-Sep	Depositions at Nottingham regarding will of Francis Thornhagh
1648	18-Oct	Francis' remains brought back and buried in Sturton le Steeple parish church

Acknowledgements

I am very grateful to Professor Martyn Bennett for reading the manuscript and sharing helpful comments and observations on it. I have also received guidance and encouragement from the many conversations I had over the course of my research with Professor Andrew Hopper, Dr David Appleby and Dr Ismini Pells. The late Mr G. M. T. Foljambe Esq. of Osberton, a direct descendant of Colonel Francis Thornhagh through the maternal line, enriched this research considerably by granting permission to use the image of the family's portrait of the Colonel in this book and also providing guidance to enquiries about the Thornhagh/Foljambe papers now deposited at the Nottinghamshire Archives Office. Glyn Hughes and Kevin Winter at the National Civil War Centre, Newark upon Trent, worked closely with me identifying and supplying permissions for a number of the images used in this book from the Centre's extensive collection. Thank you to all at the National Civil War Centre for their continued support, a place I am proud to have a long and friendly association with. A huge debt of gratitude is owed to my commissioning editor at Helion, Charles Singleton, whose advice and encouragement brought this book to fruition.

Finally this book is dedicated to the memory of my late father Brian Albert Jennings (1935–2020) who took such a great interest in my research but did not live long enough to see it published.

Introduction

Following the successful battle against the Scottish and Royalist forces outside of Preston, Lancashire in 1648, the victorious commander of the Parliamentarian forces, Oliver Cromwell, sent a report to the speaker of the House of Commons, William Lenthall. In this he provided details of the military campaign and also included a poignant commendation and praise for the commander of the Nottinghamshire horse who had been killed in the action:

Facing page: Full-size life portrait of Colonel Francis Thornhagh, *c.* 1640. Artist Unknown. (With thanks to the late G. M. T. Foljambe Esq. of Osberton for use of this image)

> I ordered Colonel Thornhaugh to command two or three regiments of horse to follow the enemy, if it were possible to make him stand till we could bring up the army. The enemy marched away 7000 or 8000 foot and about 4000 horse, we followed him with about 3000 foot and 2500 horse and dragoons; and in this prosecution that worthy gentleman Colonel Thornhaugh, pressing too boldly, was slain, being run into the body, and thigh, and head by the enemy's launcers: and give me leave to say he was a man as faithful and gallant in your service as any, and one who often heretofore lost blood in your quarrel, and now his last. He hath left some behind to inherit a father's honour, and a grieving widow – both now the interest of the commonwealth.[1]

Killed before he reached the age of 31, Francis Thornhagh, the eldest surviving son of Sir Francis Thornhagh of Fenton in Nottinghamshire, was to achieve a meteoric rise in reputation amongst Parliamentarians for both his bravery and military prowess. Cromwell's reference to the 'lost blood' of Thornhagh probably refers to the serious wounds he received in the heat of battles at Gainsborough (1643) and the second siege of Newark (1644). Henry Ireton had served as a major under him in the Nottinghamshire horse until he transferred to Cromwell's regiment after the battle of Gainsborough. Thornhagh had also served alongside, and was known to both, Colonels Cromwell and Whalley over the course of the First Civil War. Lord Fairfax himself in 1644 had sanctioned a warrant to Colonel John Hutchinson, Governor of Nottingham Castle to appoint Thornhagh 'next under Sir Thomas Fairfax, Commander-in-Chief of all the Parliamentarian horse in

1 S.C. Lomas (ed.), *The Letters and Speeches of Oliver Cromwell with Elucidations by Thomas Carlyle*, 3 vols (London: Methuen & Co, 1904), I, pp.279–85.

Nottinghamshire at all times'.[2] Over the latter part of the First Civil War, Thornhagh increasingly appears in the records of Parliament first as a soldier and later as a member of various committees. The Nottinghamshire regiment by 1644 consisted of 11 troops of horse all of whom were under the command of Thornhagh.[3] In spite of his growing reputation, his death in 1648 removed him from the subsequent events of the regicide and republic. Lucy Hutchinson saw this as a blessing for both him and his family's future prospects, as he was 'by mercy removed, so that the temptations of future times might not prevail to corrupt his pure soul'.[4] Yet between the First Civil War and his death at Preston (Chorley) he had served as one of Nottinghamshire's Members of Parliament, and had shown himself to be a committed supporter of the cause of the army against the schemes of the Presbyterian members of the House to come to an unsatisfactory compromise with the defeated King Charles I.

Eulogised at his death, esteemed in life, the short military and political career of Francis Thornhagh has failed to generate a single detailed biography of his life and military career since his death in 1648. Professor Wood had complained in 1938 about the absence of a biography observing 'Colonel Francis Thornhagh was, with the possible exception of Henry Ireton, the most brilliant soldier produced by Nottinghamshire during the civil war'.[5] Until now though, no full biography has been written.

This volume seeks to redress this omission and fill an important gap in the history of the wars as fought across both the localities and regions as well as in some of the major national battles. Using records in both national and local archives, personal recollections, family papers, contemporary pamphlets, news-sheets and accounts given of the battles by the various participants, a detailed account of Colonel Francis Thornhagh and his life has been possible and what follows seeks to tell that story.

The surname Thornhagh is spelt in a number of different ways in documents contemporary to the period: amongst the variations are Thornehagh, Thornhaugh and Thorney. In this volume the spelling most used by Colonel Francis himself in letters and documents is followed, which was Thornhagh. In contemporary sources the Nottinghamshire Horse are sometimes referred to in a shortened form as the Nottingham Horse, reflecting the town at which they were based. For the sake of continuity, throughout this work the regiment will be called the Nottinghamshire Horse but in direct quotations from contemporary sources where the phrase Nottingham Horse is used, it is retained. Original spellings are retained in all quotations from contemporary sources.

---

2 N. H. Keeble, *Lucy Hutchinson, Memoirs of the Life of Colonel Hutchinson* (London: Everyman, 1995), p.174.

3 Public Records Office (the National Archives hereafter PRO), SP 28, 174, Accounts of John Hough, Treasurer of Nottingham Parliamentary Committee.

4 Keeble, *Lucy Hutchinson*, p.225.

5 A. C. Wood, 'Colonel Francis Thornhagh', *Transactions of the Thoroton Society of Nottinghamshire*, 38 (1938), pp.82–103.

1

The Parish of Sturton and the Thornhagh Family

The American lawyer and philosopher Robert Green Ingersall (1833–1899) once said that, 'In order to appreciate a great man, we must know his surroundings. We must understand the scope of the drama in which he played – the part he acted'.[1]

To fully comprehend what made Colonel Francis Thornhagh the man he was, and the way he reacted to the great events unfolding in England over the years 1640 until his death in 1648, we first need to have an overview of the parish in which he was raised and the role of his family in the affairs of the parish and county in the decades before he was born.

The Parish of Sturton

The parish of Sturton le Steeple in the seventeenth century incorporated the deserted medieval village of west Burton and the Hamlet of Fenton, the latter the abode of the Thornhagh family. It is situated in the northeast part of the county of Nottinghamshire adjacent to the River Trent that defines the county border with Lincolnshire. The parish is situated six miles east of the market town of Retford and 6.6 miles from Gainsborough and 19.2 miles away from Lincoln, the latter two being on the other side of the river in the county of Lincolnshire. There was a bridge over the Trent at Gainsborough (a town that was to figure prominently later in the military career of Francis Thornhagh) and also a regular ferry crossing at the adjacent parish of Littleborough which lay 2.7 miles to the south-east of Sturton on the Nottinghamshire side of the Trent.

At Sturton the flat alluvial plain of the River Trent begins to ascend into the region of the Wheatley Hills, a range of high ground situated between the rivers Idle and Trent.[2] The soil is fertile and the firmer ground around Sturton,

1 R. G. Ingersall, *Great Speeches of Col. Robert Green Ingersoll* (Chicago: Rhodes & McClure, 1895).

2 J. B. Firth, *Highways and Byways of Nottinghamshire* (London: MacMillan & Co, 1924), p. 366.

The parish church of St Peter and St Paul, Sturton le Steeple. As seen across the fields from the hamlet of Fenton, the home of the Thornhagh family over the sixteenth and seventeenth centuries. (Author's photo)

nestled between the flood plains near the Trent and the more exposed land of the Wheatley high ground, had long been an attraction for early settlers. Around the village the soil is easy to plough and the higher pasture good for cattle. The ancient Roman road that ran from York to Lincoln crossed the river at Littleborough, passing through the parish of Sturton and this continued to be a major, if somewhat neglected highway through the parish over the seventeenth century.[3]

In the seventeenth century, the roads between Sturton and its neighbouring villages, generally ran across unenclosed land and where they entered a village, gates were often placed and this is probably reflected in some off the later post enclosure field names, Bolegate, Commongate and Stonegate being two examples from the parish.[4] The Norse word *gata* literally means street and so from the village tracks ran out through the gates into the surrounding districts, some even possibly being paved, thus Stonegate. Full enclosure within the parish came late compared to many adjacent parishes. The Enclosure Act for Sturton of 1823 dealt with 1940 acres (nearly half of the parish total), suggesting that open fields continued to function across much of the parish right up until the first part of the nineteenth century.[5] Even so, small areas of enclosure began to appear across the parish from the sixteenth century, possibly a number on land that the Thornhagh family owned or controlled.

The natural drainage of the parish is eastwards to the River Trent. Prior to extensive drainage schemes begun under Sir Cornelius Vermuyden in the 1630s but only substantially completed by the start of the nineteenth century, when heavy rains occurred, the amount of water flowing in the River Trent meant that water could not drain away off the land. These waters would thus spread far and wide over the land by the river lying to the east of the village of Sturton creating swamp like conditions.[6] For this reason the Romans had

3 John Ford, *The Town on the Street: Sturton-Le-Steeple* (Retford: Self Published Parish Guide, 1975), pp. 21–2.
4 Ford, *Town on the Street*, p. 25.
5 Ford, *Town on the Street*, p. 23.
6 Ford, *Town on the Street*, p. 21.

raised their original Sturton to Littleborough road on an embankment above the floodplain for about 2.5 miles. Though the original Roman road had long since disappeared by the seventeenth century, the embankments remained and carried the new track. The maintenance of this caused regular friction between the residents of the two parishes. As late as 1686, an indictment was issued at the Quarter Sessions regarding the poor condition of this stretch of highway.[7]

Stafford Bridge, which lay between the parishes of Littleborough and Sturton, was to become the focus of considerable litigation over the first part of the seventeenth century. In 1607, the parishioners of Littleborough were ordered to repair it 'before the feast of St Michael the Angel next'. By 1611 they were again in court because the said bridge was again 'greatly defective and ruinous and in great decay'. On 13 January 1615 the parishioners of Littleborough presented a petition at the Assizes in Nottingham in which they complained 'That a certain bridge called Stafford Bridge lying near the town (*sic*) of Littleborough and leading from very many Northern parts into and towards the several counties of Lincoln and Norfolk was very ruinous so that the lieges of the lord the king could not cross there without peril upon their lives'.

Lord Chief Justice Sir Edward Coke, then presiding, ruled 'it not being possible to state by whom the said bridge should be repaired', that the cost of repairs should be borne by the whole county of Nottinghamshire. This ruling didn't settle the issue though and on 15 July 1636 a new order was issued at the Assizes stating that the 'order of 13 January 1615 be cancelled and that the inhabitants of Sturton, Fenton and Littleborough shall build, maintain and repair for ever Stafford Bridge, and the whole county of Nottingham are acquitted of the burden'.[8] This whole legal process ran for nearly four decades over the seventeenth century, during which time the condition of the bridge got increasingly worse. It says something of the tenacity of the parishioners of Littleborough, and the potential cost upon them, that they fought it so long and eventually drew in their neighbours at Sturton and the resident gentry family of the Thornhaghs at Fenton to share the cost. A lot of ill will, and the potential ire of the influential Thornhagh squire, may have been generated.

The combination of large expanses of open fields and low land constantly liable to flood meant that many of Sturton's lanes became little more than tracks which were poorly maintained, potholed, rutted and in bad weather almost impassable. It was not uncommon for wagons and carts to become bogged down and in need of rescue over the cold and wet months of winter and spring. Maintenance of these highways was the responsibility of the whole parish but over much of the seventeenth century there appeared to be little money or enthusiasm to repair muddy lanes. A surviving memoir of the journey of a funeral cortege in 1645 from Fenton Hall, the home of the Thornhagh family, via Retford and ultimately on to Bolsover in Derbyshire,

---

7 H. Hampton Copnall, *Nottinghamshire County Records: Notes and Extracts from the Nottinghamshire County Records of the 17th Century* (Nottingham: Henry Saxton, 1915), p. 72.

8 Full details of these cases are provided in Copnall, *Nottinghamshire Records*, p. 84.

gives a vivid picture of travelling hardships encountered on the parish roads. It is unrecorded whether the deceased woman was either a Thornhagh member or a close relative of Sir William Cavendish. What it does suggest is that there had been a close relationship (though not of equals) between the two families, even at the time when they were then fighting on opposite sides of the then raging Civil War. This link between the families may also have been an additional reason, alongside military considerations, of Colonel Francis Thornhagh's appointment as Governor of Welbeck in August 1644 and taking on the responsibility for the two daughters of the Duke of Newcastle who were resident there then.[9] The account of that journey begins

> Finally at 8 o' clock in the morning of the 18th of November, 1645, we commenced our journey to Retford. The wain on which the body restes, was covered with black serge, on which was a low bier on which the body rested: this was pretty well secured by ropes so that no mishaps might take place on the journey – as far, at least, as human providence and foresight could divine. To this vehicle two yokes of oxen were attached and two horses in front – the oxen were deemed to be better than horses in the then very dangerous state of the roads.
>
> … The snow on the road was upwards of four inches thick, and all the ruts and hollow places were made up as level, which deceives both the drivers and the cattle, so that both were frequently down before we reached the village of Leverton [it took them over an hour to travel the 1.7 miles].
>
> … On arriving there however, it became quite evident that we should never be able to get up Cowsland without some extra assistance, and old Mr Moody offered to lend us two extra horses, which we gladly accepted.
>
> … Leaving Leverton we found the road to be in a most dreadful condition; we could not travel more than about a mile an hour, and that, too, in the midst of danger. Before we got halfway up Cowsland Hill, one of Mr Moody's horses fell and maimed itself, so that it had to betaken off and left by the side of the road, apparently in the greatest agony. Arriving at the top of the hill, we were obliged to halt for nearly half an hour, as one of the oxen had fallen lame by wrenching its claw.

Descending down the hill towards Retford, the oxen again stumbled repeatedly and the account continues. 'Near the end of Blue Stocking Lane, the wain went completely over and the coffin was overturned as well … Our grief at this mishap was quite extreme – the two female attendants [Rachel the author's wife and Abigail, her late ladyship's maid] shrieked, and our attention was directed to seeing the coffin again the right side uppermost.'

When the party finally arrived at Retford, civic dignitaries greeted and attended to them and minor damage to the coffin was repaired before setting off to the Cavendish home at Bolsover.[10]

The account of this journey in 1645 contains a number of unwitting insights into the period. Firstly, that in spite of the third siege of Newark

---

9 Alfred C. Wood, *Nottinghamshire in the Civil War* (East Ardsley: S. R. Publishers, 1971), p. 85.

10 Full report found in *The Retford & Bassetlaw Gazette,* Vol. 1, 36, 7 May 1859, a brief summary can be found in Ford, *Town on the Street*, p. 29.

beginning with two armies surrounding the town – the Scottish one being in command of much of the area the party was travelling through[11] – the cortege could not only set out assuming it was safe to do so but also that the necessary horses and oxen were available to pull the wain. Only six weeks before, Lady Thornhagh, widow (mother of Colonel Francis Thornhagh) had petitioned Parliament to 'accommodate her with a House and Furniture', presumably because of the constant hassle she was receiving at Fenton from the Royalist garrison at Newark before the siege armies were in place.[12] Secondly it illustrates just how bad the lanes could be in the autumn and that where necessary journeys were best done on horseback rather than in wagons. Wealthy families, such as the Thornhaghs, would have maintained stables with a suitable number of horses for essential travel and business. Thus from an early age, the future colonel of the Nottinghamshire horse, Francis Thornhagh, was both familiar with and competent at horsemanship. The surprising thing is that despite being desperate for mounts for his cavalry regiment, Thornhagh still kept some horses at Fenton.

The River Trent was not only a county border it was also the boundary between the religious provinces of York and Canterbury. This, coupled with the remoteness of many parishes in the north of the county beyond the town of Newark, facilitated the early arrival and establishment of Puritanism in this part of the county. It was particularly strong in the parishes of Scrooby, Scaftworth, and Worksop and also across the river at Gainsborough. In fact many Nottinghamshire Puritans worshipped at Gainsborough, using the boundary to mask their activity and so only be reported for being absent from church to the Church Courts in the archdeaconry of Nottingham rather than the more serious crime of meeting in illegal conventicles. The parish of Sturton made its own contribution to the rise of separatism with two of the main leaders, John Robinson and John Smith both being born and raised within the parish and educated by the committed Protestant curate of the village church (until 1602) John Quyppe. Their unlicensed preaching activities over the years 1605–1608 in and around Sturton drew many away from their own parish churches to hear them. On 12 January 1608, the churchwardens of South Leverton, two miles south of Sturton were presented at the church courts for allowing John Robinson to preach in their pulpit. A month later the churchwardens at the adjacent parish of Treswell were also presented for the same offence.[13] It seems most likely that many of John Robinson's extended family and friends would have travelled from Sturton to hear their local celebrity. Certainly a number of Sturton residents are presented for being absent from their church over the first decade of the seventeenth century but whether they were 'sermon gadding' or recusants is unclear. By 1610 the more extreme of the Puritans

11 Stuart B. Jennings, 'The Third and Final Siege of Newark (1645–1646) and the Impact of the Scottish Army upon Nottinghamshire and the Surrounding Counties, *Midland History*, 37:2 (2012), pp.142–62.

12 Journal of the House of Commons (hereafter HC Journal), (London: HMSO, 1802), IV, 20 September 1645, p. 281.

13 Nottingham University Manuscripts Department (hereafter NUMD), Archdeaconry of Nottingham Act Books, A24.

(the separatists) had fled the county to Holland to avoid persecution but many of their extended families still remained in this part of the county. The attitude of the Thornhagh family over the first four decades to the Puritan phenomena is difficult to gauge. One suspects that providing individuals kept a low profile and observed the required deference toward them, they overlooked a great deal. The fact that Sir Francis Thornhagh and his son Francis quickly sided with Parliament in 1642, with little persuading, and in 1643 Sir Francis raised a regiment of cavalry and Francis junior commanded it suggests that both had an understanding and sympathy for the constitutional and religious issues that divided Parliament from the King in the civil wars in the mid seventeenth century.[14]

Estimating the population of Sturton, and its hamlet of Fenton, in the seventeenth century is fraught with difficulties. There are no census details for the period and surviving documents were usually generated for the purpose of taxation and tithes rather than counting the population. This is further complicated by the fact that church registers for the parish are lost until 1638 and incomplete for periods over the time of the civil wars. The best source for estimating population numbers is likely to be the somewhat latter 1664 and 1674 Hearth Tax returns. Both of these appear to be complete for the parish and list both those liable for the tax of 2s for every hearth, and also those exempted on the grounds of poverty and need. They list households and their heads for the parish, including identifying those homes that are vacant at the time. According to the historian John Beckett, for Nottinghamshire parishes a multiplier of 4.25 per household is not an unreasonable figure to use to arrive at an approximate population. This allows for the fact that some may be much larger with children and servants whilst others may only consist of one or two persons.[15] In 1664, 126 households in both Sturton and Fenton were identified. The largest number of hearths counted in any one dwelling was recorded at the house of John Thorney (Thornhagh) Esquire. The number of households suggests a population of around 530 within the parish at the time of the assessment. A decade later, in 1674, the number of households recorded was 16 for Fenton and 75 for Sturton, giving a total of 91 for the parish. This suggests a population for that date of around 387 for the parish. There had, therefore, been a reduction of 35 households across the parish. Interestingly though, the number of hearths recorded at John Thorney's house had risen to 22, suggesting resurgence in the family's fortunes. In 1664, John was only 17 and still under guardianship and Fenton Hall had served purely as a dowager house until the death of his grandmother in 1661.[16] Ten years later he was back at Fenton taking full control of the family estate.

---

14 For a more detailed examination of Puritanism in Nottinghamshire see S.B. Jennings, *'The Gathering of the Elect': The Development, Nature and Socio-Economic Structures of Protestant Religious Dissent in Seventeenth Century Nottinghamshire* (Unpublished PhD Thesis, Nottingham Trent University, 1999).

15 W. F. Webster (ed.), *Nottinghamshire Hearth Tax Returns 1664:1674*, Thoroton Record Series, XXXVII (1896), pp. vii–xlii.

16 Wood, 'Francis Thornhagh', p. *82*.

The 10-pinnacled tower of St Peter and St Paul, a familiar sight on the skyline and the parish church to the Thornhagh family. (Author's photo)

The Hearth Tax figures suggest that over the course of the second half of the seventeenth century, as the Thornhagh fortunes rose, the population of the parish slowly declined. Two factors possibly contributed to this trend, the first being an increase in the amount of dairy farming across the parish. By the eighteenth century Trent Side cheese, produced in and around Sturton had become a much-desired product and sold in great quantities at the Nottingham Goose Fair and at markets at Gainsborough and Retford. In 1764, due to inflation, the price of cheese rose by a third to 8d per pound, which took it beyond the means of ordinary citizens and led to the infamous cheese riots of that year at the Goose Fair.[17] The second factor related to enclosure, although at Sturton this proceeded much slower than in neighbouring parishes, it was happening frequently enough to encourage the migration of some of the smaller cottagers away from the village. With reduced common to graze their cow upon and less labour required for dairy farming, times became increasingly hard for the smaller cottager.

At the heart of much of the changes explored above, would have been the Thornhagh estate and it is to the history of that family prior to the birth of our subject, Francis, we now turn to complete our understanding of the surroundings that shaped him.

The Thornhagh Family

By the time of Francis Thornhagh's birth in 1617, the family presence at the hamlet of Fenton lying over half a mile southeast of Sturton, extended back nearly 200 years. Local historians such as Alfred Wood have tentatively suggested that the roots of this local family may stretch back even further to the thirteenth century with individuals of that name being involved in the affairs of Lincoln. They first acquired land at Fenton by the marriage of John Thornhagh to Katherine Paine (Payne) of Fenton in the late 1430s.[18]

The absence of early parish registers for Sturton – those surviving begin in 1638 – makes the specific dating of family events very difficult. Often it is stray references in wills, inquisitions and county administrative records that enable us to provide an approximate chronology. Subsequent to the marriage of John and Katherine, there followed six generations of healthy male heirs all reaching adulthood until the arrival of Francis in 1617, meaning that the family not only became well established but also prospered.

17 Peter Wilkes, *The Great Nottingham Goose Fair* (Burton-on-Trent: Trent Valley Publications, 1989), p. 15.

18 Wood, 'Francis Thornhagh', p. 82.

In the sixteenth century the Thornhagh estates were greatly enhanced by the marriage of John (d. 1613) to Elizabeth Bailles (Baills) around 1566. She was the daughter of Brian Bailles, a wealthy merchant of Potters Newton near Leeds. The death of Elizabeth's only brother William, without an heir, meant that the whole of his estate came through Elizabeth to the Thornhagh family. In 1600, the family's rising status was further reflected by John's appointment as the Earl of Rutland's deputy and Lieutenant for Sherwood Forest.[19] Sir John died towards the end of 1613/4 and in his will dated 13 January 1613/4 he left his estate to his son John (then aged 47 years) and made cash bequests of £2,240 to his daughters and grandchildren. To his two daughters =he left each £20 'in full satisfaction of their portion' but £1000 to his grandson Francis, £700 to his granddaughter Elizabeth and a further £500 to his younger grandchild Bridget. The inquisition post mortem dated 24 March 1614 recorded 'one capitall messuage or Tenemt in Fenton called Fenton Hall', 200 acres of land, 120 acres of meadow, 200 acres of 'pasture and common pasture for all working cattell in Fenton, Sturton and Littleborough'. They also recorded the manor of Oswalbeck 'in free socage, by Fealty' and also a number of other lands held by lease from either the king or other gentlemen for either periods of years or for life. These latter lands were appraised as being worth in total £23.6s.8d.[20] Although well below the wealth of the county's aristocratic families, by the start of the seventeenth century, the Thornhaghs were firmly established in the group of Nottinghamshire's significant landed gentry families.

The son, also John (1567–1627) served as a cadet in the Manners household at Belvoir Castle and was knighted by James I in 1603. He served as a magistrate over the period 1603–1626 and High Sheriff of Nottingham 1617–1618. He died in 1627 and was succeeded by his son Francis (1593–1643), the future father of Colonel Francis Thornhagh.

It was during the lifetime of Sir Francis that the family's future political path was shaped by events at Westminster. He had been knighted in 1615 and served, like his father, as a Justice of the Peace over the years 1626–1637 and as High Sheriff of Nottingham, 1637–1638. Thus Sir Francis held significant offices within the county over a period of national, social and political upheaval. These included the drainage of the Isle of Axholme by the commissioning of Sir Cornelius Vermuyden (1596–1677) in 1626 by Charles I. Sir Francis was High Sheriff and responsible for the allocation and collection of the controversial 'Ship Money' levy over the years 1636 and 1637. Two surviving incidents recorded in the records give us an insight into how two of these issues, drainage and Ship Money, impacted on the life and actions of the family.

In 1630, the Quarter Sessions Justices meeting at Retford, wrote to the Privy Council about an assault on Sir Francis Thornhagh's tenant or servants by workmen of Sir Cornelius Vermuyden. A deposition by Mary Thornhill was sent to the council:

19 Ford, *Town on the Street*, p. 36.

20 Nottinghamshire Archives (hereafter NA), Inquisition Post Mortem of John Thornhagh of Fenton, Esq., 23 March 1614, DD/FJ/4/17/1.

> On the fifth of August the deponents going into a close of Francis Thornhill where John Molanus, a Dutch man with eight others, had wrongfully entered and digged, after divers speeches Molanus struck the said Edward (son of Mary) and offered to strike the said Mary, and afterwards used wrongful and indecent words against Sir Francis Thornhagh.[21]

By then the initial drainage scheme of the Isle of Axholme, bordering Nottinghamshire, Lincolnshire and Yorkshire, was drawing towards a close but reoccurring flooding at west Stockwith in Nottinghamshire had led Vermuyden's workmen further down the River Trent to undertake remedial works. Whatever the reason, such behaviour and exchange of words towards the gentry of the region, even if the scheme carried the king's warrant, were deemed to be destructive of good order and deference within the shire. It would have done little to warm Sir Francis's attitude towards the actions of those appointed by the King, though it was never expressed as such.

In the Ship Money assessment of 1636, which Thornhagh inherited as he began his term as High Sheriff in 1637, Retford was rated at £30, Nottingham at £200 and Newark at £120. In 1637, it became clear to Sir Francis that Newark would not be able to meet its assessment. His knowledge of the region, especially Retford, encouraged him to write to the Privy Council in 1637 suggesting that Retford was able to pay £50 more and that the same amount be reduced off the sum that was levied on Newark. Retford enjoyed a privileged status which had led to its under-assessment but Sir Francis wasn't going to allow that to create friction within the county, even though the King's tax had to be met.[22] Some of the shire's inhabitants proved to be slow in paying their Ship Money dues and Sir Francis 'was driven to talk of distraining in order to force them to disgorge.' During Thornhagh's time as High Sheriff all the moneys assessed were raised but by 1639 the relationship between court and county had broken down completely and £2,786 of the county assessment of £3,500 remained unpaid.[23] Whether Sir Francis refused to pay in 1639 remains unclear from the surviving records but his sympathies towards the concerns of both the short and long parliaments of 1640 are clear.

On completion of his term of office as High Sheriff at the end of 1638, Sir Francis appears to disappear from any administrative or governmental office within the shire. He is not reappointed to the list of magistrates for Nottinghamshire, a role not picked up by his son until 1642. It may possibly be the case that his health was frail after holding office and he needed some time on his estate at Fenton for recuperation. He may also have had to use this time to consolidate the fortunes of the family estate, with his son and heir being overseas undertaking military service. On his son's return in 1640 and subsequent marriage, it is the son Francis who represents the growing Parliamentarian sentiment of Nottingham (see Chapter 3), but is unlikely to have been able to do so without, at the least, the tacit approval of his

21 Calendar of State Papers Domestic (hereafter CSPD), 1629–31 (London: HMSO, 1860), 8 October 1630, p. 355.

22 CSPD, 1635–36, 253; 1636–1637, 288; 1637, 158. See also PRO, SP 16/347/75.

23 Wood, *Nottinghamshire Civil War*, p. 11.

father. That Sir Francis was seen as a supporter of Parliament is shown by his appointment, along with his son, to serve on the committee for the defence of the town by an ordinance dated 15 December 1642.[24] A few days later, Sir Francis was requested in a militia ordinance to raise a regiment of horse, to which he agreed and appointed his son Francis to be the regiment's lieutenant colonel responsible for raising, equipping and training the recruited troops. Within four months of receiving his military commission, Sir Francis was dead, dying on 28 April 1643 and being buried alongside his late father in the chancel of Sturton parish church.

This then is the surroundings, both geographical and familial, in which Colonel Francis Thornhagh was raised and nurtured, and it is to his story that the rest of this book now turns.

24 HC Journal, II, p. 909; Wood, *Nottinghamshire Civil War*, p. 124.

2

The Early Years of Francis Thornhagh, 1617–1642

According to information supplied by Gervase Piggot of Thrumpton at the Nottinghamshire Visitations 1662–1664, Francis Thornhagh was born in 1617. He was the second son of Sir Francis Thornhagh and his wife Jane, though an elder brother John had died in infancy. He also had three younger brothers, Henry, John and Anthony. It is unclear whether Francis or his sister Jane was the eldest child.[1] The absence of both parish registers and bishop's transcripts for this period makes it impossible to be sure or even to arrive at a date or month for the birth of Francis. What is certain is that by the early 1620s Fenton Hall would have been a busy household with six children, servants, nanny, estate manager and a constant stream of visitors to see Sir Francis about business, county administrative issues or social calls. Gervase Piggot will figure prominently in the story of Francis Thornhagh later in this book.

Early Years and Education

The initial education of Francis is not known but may well have involved a private tutor at Fenton during his very early years. At around the age of seven he would have been sent to the Free Grammar School at Lincoln. In her biography of her husband John Hutchinson, Lucy Hutchinson speaks of John as being there 'soon after he had left off long coats'. This suggests around the age of seven or eight.[2] Although Francis was two years younger than John, he would have probably gone to the school around the same age of eight and probably boarded there. Francis and John did meet up at the school and in spite of the age difference became lifelong friends from this time. As Lincoln was only 20 miles away it is very likely that over the holidays and occasional weekends, Francis returned home to Fenton where he would be introduced to the administrations of the estate and in particular the care and use of the

1 K. S. S. Train (ed.), 'Nottinghamshire Visitations, 1662–1664', *Thoroton Society Record Series*, XIII (1950), p. 67.

2 Keeble, *Lucy Hutchinson*, p. 39, p. 347.

Engraving of Lucy Hutchinson, whose *Memoirs* of her husband Colonel John Hutchinson make considerable reference to Francis Thornhagh. Engraver unknown. (Author's collection)

many horses in the family stables. These were needed for his father's many journeys around the county both for business and service as a magistrate. Thus at an early age he developed both his horsemanship skills and his love of horses, interests that would not be out of place in the life of a young gentleman. These, plus his knowledge of the region gained as he travelled regularly to Gainsborough, Lincoln, Retford, Newark and later, when older, Nottingham were to serve him well when the civil war began in 1642. A number of these places were to figure later in his military career.

The Lincoln Free Grammar school had been created in 1584 when the city council amalgamated the ancient grammar school with the cathedral school, both of which had been struggling to cope financially and deliver an education satisfactory to the parents who sent their children to either. This produced a single school with good resources and ensured that both a master and an usher could continue to be employed. Only an admission fee was charged for students to attend, 6d for the younger boys to be taught by the usher or 1s when placed under the care of the master. Given the Thornhagh family status, it is most likely that Francis was always directly under the supervision of the master. To be admitted to the school though, each boy had to be able to show that he was of an ability to cope with the school syllabus, and this was probably undertaken by examination.[3] As with most grammar schools of this time, Latin would have dominated the syllabus and a mixture of memorising and repetition were used to teach the scholars. As noted above, a boy would usually enter the school around the ages of seven or eight and over the next six or seven years acquire a sufficient grounding in Latin to be able to attend university. At university this concentration on a classical education continued to be stressed with a focus on subjects such as rhetoric, logic, philosophy, the classics, mathematics and theology. These were considered necessary disciplines for creating a true 'gentlemen'. At the grammar school, the days for scholars were very long. They would begin at six in the morning and during the summer continue through to six in the evening, with short breaks for breakfast and dinner. Holiday periods for the boys varied from school to school but where usually between five to eight weeks spread across the year.[4]

We know something about life at the school and its master when Francis was present through the Memoirs of Lucy Hutchinson, whose husband's

3 R. Gurnham, *A History of Lincoln* (Chichester: Phillimore, 2009), pp. 99–100.

4 J. A. Sharpe, *Early Modern England: A Social History, 1550–1760* (London: Arnold, 1997), pp. 272–4.

time at the school overlapped. We know that at the school 'there was a master very famous for learning and piety, Mr Clarke; but he was such a supercilious pedant, and so conceited of his own pedantic forms, that he gave Mr Hutchinson a disgust of him, and he profited very little there'.[5] One can imagine many of the boys finding learning there very tedious and taxing, but Francis certainly learnt enough to be able subsequently to move on to Magdalen College, Oxford.

Lucy Hutchinson identified an additional subject taught at the Free Grammar School, which both Francis Thornhagh and John Hutchinson enjoyed and shared in together:

> An old Low-country soldier was entertained to train them in arms, and they all brought themselves weapons; and instead of childish sports, when they were not at their books, were exercised in all their military postures, and in assaults and defences; which instructions were not useless in a few years after to some of them; and Colonel Thornhagh, who was trained in this sportive militia with Colonel Hutchinson, afterwards was his fellow soldier in earnest, when the great cause of God's and England's rights came to be disputed with swords against encroaching princes.[6]

University and Inns of Court

At the age of seventeen, Francis matriculated at Magdalen College, Oxford on 8 May 1635 and just over a year later, in November 1636, he was admitted as a member of the Inner Temple, one of the four Inns of Court at London.[7] In the seventeenth century, gentlemen scholars could be admitted to either Cambridge or Oxford colleges up to three years earlier than scholars in the twenty first century. It has been estimated that the average age of entry for the elder sons of gentry families was 16.6 years and that barely a fifth of elder sons bothered to graduate.[8] There is no record of Francis graduating and in so many ways he reflects the fashion of the times. He was acquiring enough of a classical education during his time at university to serve the requirements of a gentleman. As a fresher/schoolboy fellow he would have begun with acquiring the required skills in the *Trivium* (grammar, logic and rhetoric) before moving on to the *Quadrivium* (arithmetic, geometry, music and astronomy). Unless you were following a course of professional studies such as divinity, law or medicine, this was the syllabus that all undergraduates followed.[9]

5 Keeble, *Lucy Hutchinson*, p. 39.
6 Keeble, *Lucy Hutchinson*, p. 47.
7 J. Foster (ed.), *Alumni Oxonienses, 1500–1714* (Oxford: Oxford University Press, 1891)
8 P. Wallis and C. Webb, 'The Education and Training of Gentry Sons in Early Modern England', *London School of Ecomomics, Economic History Department Working Papers*, WP128 (London: LSE, 2009), pp. 17–21.
9 For a detailed examination of the subject see J. W. Adamson, 'The Seventeenth Century Curriculum', in *The Cambridge History of English and American Literature in 18 Volumes* (Cambridge: Cambridge University Press, 1907–21) IX, Chapter 15, Education.

A code of conduct for scholars written down for Trinity College, Cambridge by James Duport in 1660 has survived to this day and may possibly reflect the sort of discipline expected of scholars across both Universities throughout the first part of the seventeenth century. In it we are given a glimpse of the aspirations, if not always the reality, of what many masters expected from their students. Scholars were instructed to 'turn up for prayers on time' and advised 'to spend the Lord's Day wholly in religious duties'. They were also instructed 'never go into the town, except to ye church or schools or booksellers or book-binders shop' and also to avoid within their college 'gadding and gossiping from chamber to chamber'.[10] This environment proved to be very restrictive to some undergraduates and a number often got into trouble with either the town authorities or their college masters. It probably suited the more disciplined life-style and religious temperament of Francis Thornhagh though, but he wasn't averse to either laughter or friendship. As Lucy Hutchinson recalled of him when they first met in the early 1640s: 'He was of a most excellent good nature to all men, and zealous for his friends; he wanted counsel and deliberation, and was sometimes too facile to flatterers, but had judgement enough to discern his errors when they were represented to him and worth enough not to persist in an injurious mistake because he had once entertained it.'[11]

His character, so extolled in the passage above, was probably formed early in life and gently refined over the period of his late teens.

When gentry sons went to the Inns of Court, on average, they were around 19.8 years and Francis was certainly around this age, possibly younger, when he entered the Inner Temple.[12] Here he would acquire enough knowledge of the law to be able to administer the estates to which he was heir and also perform adequately duties as a magistrate, advised by the session's resident lawyer, if or when appointed to serve. Given the Thornhagh family's status within Nottinghamshire, such an appointment was seen as inevitable once a space on the bench became available as it did for Francis in 1642.[13]

Military Service in the Netherlands

The thrill of the basic military training that Francis received at school never left him and around the age of 21 he sought to build upon that experience by travelling to the Netherlands to serve with the Dutch army during the Franco-Spanish War (1635–1659).[14] This was most likely over the years 1638–1639, as a comprehensive list of English gentleman present at the Siege of Breda in 1637 fails to identify him as being present at that event.[15]

10 'Cambridge University guide from 350 years ago', <https:www.bbc.co.uk/news/uk-england-cambridgeshire-24461814>, accessed 15 January 2019.

11 Keeble, *Lucy Hutchinson*, p. 98.

12 Wallis & Webb, 'Education of Gentry Sons', p.17.

13 Copnall, *Nottinghamshire County Records*, p. 9.

14 Wood, 'Francis Thornhagh', pp. 85–6.

15 I am indebted to Dr Ismini Pell of Leicester University for sharing this information from her own research.

Although no record of his military service survives, it is almost certain that he would have become acquainted with both the Dutch and Swedish military innovations developed over the earlier part of the Thirty Years' War (1618–1648). He would have seen at first hand the importance of drill, developed by the Dutch under Maurice of Nassau, in enhancing efficient tactical flexibility in the midst of battle. This was not only at the regimental level but also in the creation of smaller but more professional armies. He probably also had the chance to witness the new use of cavalry regiments developed by the Swedish forces. This involved using the force of the charge of horse by making the first three ranks of riders smashed into the ranks of the enemy with their swords in their hands and reserving the firing of their pistols for close quarters and the pursuit. This was in complete contrast with previous practice where cavalry rode up in ranks to within pistol range of the enemy, discharging their pistols and retiring for the next rank to come forward and repeat the action.[16] Surviving accounts of the engagement of the Nottinghamshire horse with Prince Rupert's forces at the second siege of Newark (1644) strongly suggest that Thornhagh adopted a Swedish-type charge against the Royalist forces but failed to break their ranks (see Chapter 3). The limited military experience of Francis Thornhagh on the Continent was judged to be exceptional enough for his father to appoint him lieutenant colonel of the Nottinghamshire Horse during its recruitment at the beginning of 1643 and to take immediate command of after the death of his father, Sir Francis, in April 1643.[17]

Marriage, Kinship and Evolving Political Links

By 1640, Francis was back in Nottingham, partly for personal reasons but also to support his father in the deteriorating political situation in England. Although there is no clear evidence, it seems likely that Sir Francis Thornhagh's health was deteriorating, resulting in his death at the age of 49 in 1643. In the opening months of 1642 it was the son Francis who appeared to have taken up a lot of the physical work across the county and with the Commons seeking to consolidate a strong Parliamentarian support within Nottingham, he proved to be their man.

The main event for Francis in 1640 appears to have been the arrangement of a marriage contract between the families of the Thornhaghs at Fenton and the St Andrews of Gotham. By the end of the year, but probably before the season of Advent, Francis was married to Elizabeth, the second daughter and co-heiress of John St Andrew of Gotham. After they were wed they established their family home in the St Mary's Hill district of Nottingham, though his wife still retained Rushcliffe Hall at Gotham.[18] Their Nottingham residence was to be the family home up until 1662 when Francis' son John inherited

16 See I. Gentles, 'The Civil Wars in England', in J. Kenyon & J. Ohlmeyer (eds), *The Civil Wars: A Military History, 1638–1660* (Oxford: Oxford University Press, 1998), pp. 103–33.

17 Wood, *Nottinghamshire Civil War*, p. 32.

18 Wood, 'Francis Thornhagh', p. 86.

the estate at Fenton on the death of his grandmother the dowager Jane. In the year 1678, John finally sold the Nottingham house and subsequently brought the manor of Osberton from William Lake in 1682.[19] A record of events over those early years of marriage can be ascertained by the submission of Gervase Pigott on behalf of the family at the Heraldic Visitation to Nottinghamshire in 1662. Within a year of the marriage their first daughter, Elizabeth, was born followed by the birth of a second daughter, Jane, who was born in 1643 and baptised at St Peters in Nottingham on 4 May in that year.[20] A son and heir for Francis, John, was born in 1647 and was probably less than a year old when his father was killed at the battle of Preston.[21] Gervase Pigott had married Mary, the older sister of Elizabeth, the wife of Francis, so the two men were brothers in law as well as strong supporters of the Parliament during the war. It also appears that Pigott was named as the guardian of Francis Thornhagh's children in the Colonel's will of 1648 and was still acting in that capacity in 1662 as John Thornhagh was still only 15 at the time of visitation. By then the widow of Colonel Francis had remarried a distant cousin, William Skeffington around the year 1655.[22]

The marriage of Francis was to cement further the relationships of both blood and friendship across a number of individuals who went on to serve Parliament in the forthcoming civil wars. Gervase Pigott served as a member of the Nottinghamshire committee and later as an MP. John Hutchinson, life-long friend of Francis, served as the Governor and Colonel of Nottingham castle and Hutchinson's cousin Henry Ireton served as a major under Thornhagh in the Nottingham horse until after the battle of Gainsborough of 1643. All three men were influential in supporting Hutchinson in his disagreements with a number of the town's civic leaders over the course of the war. Thornhagh (b. 1617) and Ireton (b. 1613) attended Oxford whilst Hutchinson (b. 1613) went to Cambridge and all three had gone on to study law at London. Lucy Hutchinson judged all four men to be of a puritan disposition in regard to religion and honest, sober and trustworthy in their service to Parliament.[23] Unlike the other three gentlemen, Ireton had no family commitments in 1642 and so felt able to leave Nottinghamshire in that year to join the Parliamentarian army assembling under the command of the Earl of Essex. He was present at the battle of Edgehill in October of that year.

The Road to War in Nottinghamshire, 1641–1642

The actions and activities of Francis Thornhagh over the two years leading up to the outbreak of the civil war are somewhat obscure, with only a few occasional references surviving in both local and national records. Settling

19 Ford, *Town on the Street*, p. 37.

20 NA, Parish Register of St Peters Nottingham, PR, 3630, 4 May 1643.

21 Train, 'Nottinghamshire Visitations', p. 67.

22 Ford, *Town on the Street*, p. 37. See also the monument to John St Andrew (d. 1625) and his wife in Gotham Parish church, which records genealogical details of his children and grandchildren.

23 Keeble, *Lucy Hutchinson*, pp. 75–6, pp. 98–9.

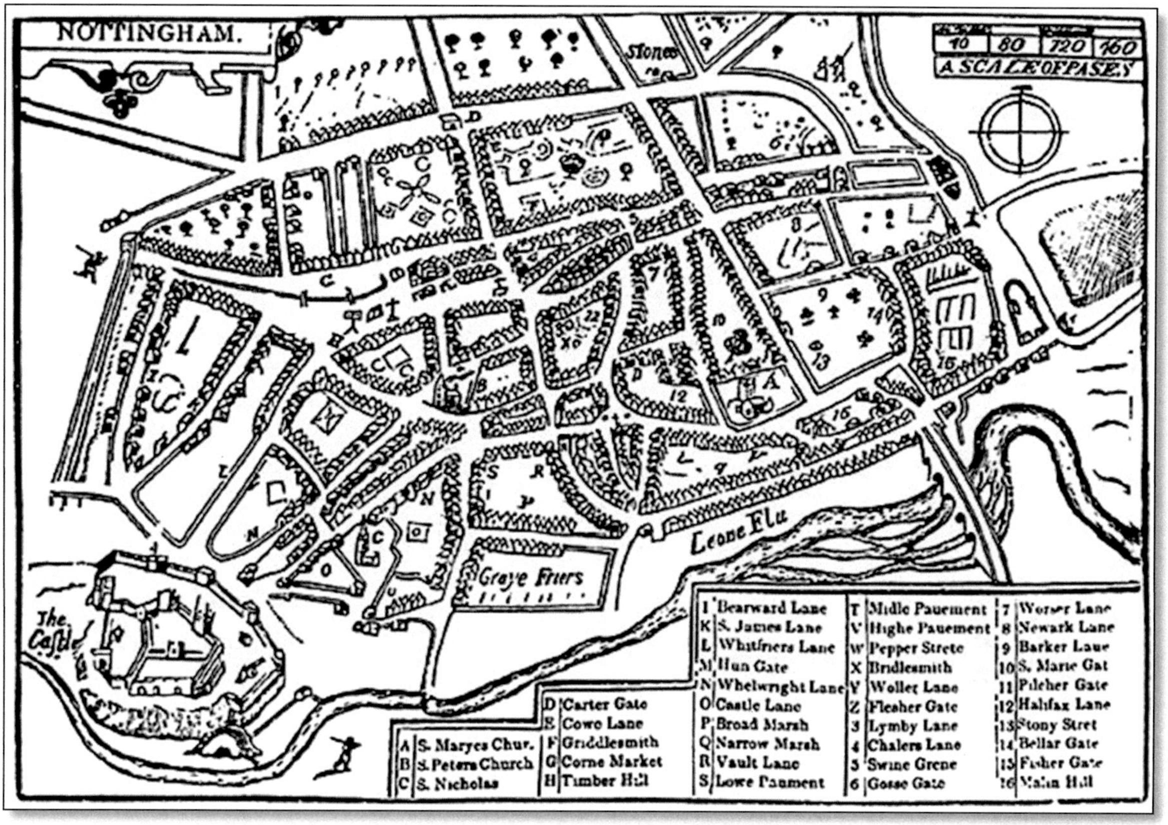

Detail from John Speed's map of Nottinghamshire, 1610, showing the town of Nottingham at the start of the seventeenth century. (Author's collection)

into married life, picking up some of the reins of family responsibility after his adventures overseas with the Dutch army, and the birth of his first child probably occupied much of the year 1641. Two petitions were sent up to Parliament from Nottinghamshire in 1641. The first expressed continuing support for the established church and its bishops and was signed by one nobleman, five knights, over a hundred 'gentlemen of quality', all the clergy and over 6,000 commoners. A second quickly followed, complaining of the 'grievances under the ecclesiastical government of archbishops, bishops & c.' with over 1,500 esquires and gentlemen signing this petition.[24] This later petition most likely bore the signatures of Thornhagh (father and son), Hutchinson, Ireton and many other prominent families who were later to serve the cause of Parliament.

At the start of 1642, Thornhagh was still adjudged neutral enough by the crown to be appointed to the bench of Nottinghamshire magistrates.[25] Thereafter though, his sympathies to the cause of Parliament became increasingly clear. In February 1642, Thornhagh and Ireton together carried up to London a petition from Nottinghamshire to the House. The contents of this petition have not survived, but the response suggests it was one of support for the two Houses. In the drawing up of this petition, considerable

24 Wood, *Nottinghamshire Civil War*, p. 12.

25 Copnall, *Nottinghamshire County Records*, p. 9.

Charles I raises his standard at Nottingham on 22 August 1642, rallying his supporters to military service for their King. Engraver Thomas Bauer after C. W. Cope. (Author's collection)

opposition was encountered from a local sergeant of law, Gilbert Boone of Hockerton. Such was the intensity of the sergeant's actions that it was felt necessary for the two men to personally deliver the petition to Parliament. After considering the document, both Ireton and Thornhagh were summoned to appear before the house where the Speaker, William Lenthall, thanked them for their 'care of the Commonwealth, and of Respect to this House: and of judgement in discovery of this man: For which he was commanded to return you Thanks'.[26]

In March 1642, a further petition signed by 4,540 knights, gentlemen, freeholders, the Mayor and aldermen of Nottingham was presented by a large deputation from the shire, including John Hutchinson, to the King himself who at the time was at York. This respectfully requested the monarch return to London to further encourage renewed conversations with both Houses of Parliament. Sir Francis Thornhagh, and his son Francis, were both signatories to this petition but it is unlikely that either of them were part of the deputation that went to York.[27] Sir Francis's health was too fragile for him

26 HC Journal, II, 28 February 1642, p. 458.
27 Wood, *Nottinghamshire Civil War*, p. 12.

to undertake the journey and Francis was probably still at London or on his journey back to Nottingham.

In the first week of August, the Lord Lieutenant Lord Newark and the Sheriff Lord Digby rode into Nottingham with a troop of horse with the intention of seizing the county magazine for the King. In this action they had completely misjudged the prevailing mood of the town and a large crowd of the town's gentry and freeholders gathered outside the building to stop them from so doing. It is very likely that Francis Thornhagh was part of that crowd of prominent citizens who successfully thwarted this attempt on the county's main resource for its defence. The King arrived in Nottingham later that month and raised his standard at Nottingham castle on 22 August 1642, thus calling his retainers and supporters to rally to his cause, though fighting had already begun in some parts of the country. Francis would have wisely kept a low profile over this period, perhaps even returning to his wife's house at Gotham or his father's estate at Fenton. As a young active man, with military experience overseas he would have made an ideal recruit (even if under duress) for the King's fledgling army.[28]

After the battle of Edgehill in October, John Hutchinson, with the assistance of some troops supplied by Sir John Gell of Derby and a number of the town's gentry seized Nottingham Castle to stop it from falling into the hands of the King's supporters. Francis Thornhagh was almost certainly one of those who supported Hutchinson in this action. Thereafter things escalated quickly towards the end of 1642. On 29 December 1642, Parliament appointed a Committee for the Defence of Nottingham, whose membership included both Sir Francis and his son Francis.[29] In that same month Sir Francis Thornhagh agreed to a military ordinance of Parliament to raise a regiment of horse and accept a commission to the rank of colonel. He quickly appointed his son Francis as his second in command and commissioned him to the rank of lieutenant colonel.[30]

28 See Wood, *Nottinghamshire Civil War*, pp. 17–29.

29 HC Journal, II, 29 December 1642, p. 905.

30 See especially Wood, *Nottinghamshire Civil War*, chapter IV.

3

The Civil War: Halting the Royalist Advance, 1643–1644

Over the first four months of 1643, Francis Thornhagh quickly found himself taking increasing responsibility for both training and equipping the regiment and its military activities. At the same time he was also supporting his mother and securing the family estate at Fenton following the death of his father, Sir Francis, in April 1643. Nottinghamshire found itself at the forefront of the King's three-prong plan to move his forces towards London and take the capital. A Royalist army, under the command of the then Earl of Newcastle, a Nottinghamshire peer, was moving down from Yorkshire to support the King's army at Oxford by taking control of the North and the Midlands, and threatening the Parliamentarian Eastern Association territory. A third Royalist army was moving towards the capital from the southwest. With Royalist forces encroaching upon the heartland of Nottinghamshire: Newcastle in Yorkshire, Henderson at Newark and Henry Hastings (later Lord Loughborough) based at Ashby-de-la-Zouch; the Parliamentarian forces based at Nottingham needed to act quickly to secure their survival. This chapter explores the role of Francis Thornhagh and his regiment of horse in stemming the Royalist advance.

Training, Equipping and Maintaining the Regiment

Within seven days of Charles raising his royal standard at Nottingham, Parliament issued the following order:

> That Sir Francis Thornhagh, and Hardolfe Wasthenes (sic), shall be appointed Treasures, to receive such monies and plate as shall come in upon the subscriptions in the county of Nottingham, and shall send them to Hull, to Sir Jo. Hotham.
>
> … And it is further ordered, that they shall be likewise Commissaries to value such Horses as shall be brought in upon the said subscriptions.[1]

1 HC Journal, II, 29 August 1642, p. 743.

Hardolph Wasteneys does not appear in any other documentation, either local or national afterwards and died in 1649, and so many local historians have tended to assume that he never took up the appointment or was nothing more than a passive supporter of the Parliamentarian cause. This left most of the administrative duties on the shoulders of Sir Francis until his death in 1643.[2] It also appears, that the Thornhaghs, both father and son, were recognised as having some knowledge of horses, and of the horse trade market which was, prior to the war, expanding within Nottinghamshire.[3] This was recognised by Parliament as being useful for the provisioning of horse for the fledgling Parliamentarian forces then being formed. Sir Francis Thornhagh may possibly have helped the securing of additional horses for the troop of cavalry Henry Ireton raised within Nottingham and which fought under the Earl of Essex against the Royalists at the battle of Edgehill on 25 October 1642.[4] It is not surprising therefore that in December 1642 Sir Francis Thornhagh was awarded a commission by Parliament to raise a regiment of cavalry of which he was to be the colonel. The presence of his son Francis at Nottingham provided him with an experienced and trusted soldier to serve as his second in command bearing the rank of lieutenant colonel.

According to many of the military manuals of the early seventeenth century, a regiment of horse ideally should consist of around 600 men divided into six troops. The reality over the period of the civil war was to prove to be very different across the county though. The high costs involved in raising, equipping and maintaining such a regiment often meant they were smaller in size than the ideal. In many regional armies a troop of horse might consist of anything from 30 to 60 mounted men, forming regiments of only between 180 to 360 troopers.[5] The raising of a troop or regiment of horse presented very particular problems compared to that of a regiment of foot. Colonels needed to recruit both officers and soldiers who had a degree of knowledge about animal management as well as the ability to be trained in tactical and military skills. Initially it was hoped that recruits would bring their own horses, meaning that some of the early units, especially Royalist, were made up of men drawn predominantly from gentry or yeoman backgrounds. As already noted above though, from the end of August Sir Francis was acquiring horses from across Nottinghamshire for the use of Parliament and it was unlikely therefore that suitable recruits identified within Nottinghamshire were turned away for the lack of a horse. This possibly gave the Nottinghamshire horse a body of troopers drawn from a variety of social backgrounds, which was only bettered by Cromwell's regiment of horse (Ironsides). The officer corp of the Nottinghamshire horse, though, was drawn almost exclusively from the gentry class.

2 Wood, *Nottinghamshire Civil War*, p. 125.

3 P. R. Edwards, 'The Supply of Horses to the Parliamentarian and Royalist Armies in the English Civil War', *History Research*, 65, issue 165 (February, 1995), pp. 49–66.

4 Wood, *Nottinghamshire Civil War*, p. 27.

5 G. Markham, *The Souldiers Accident* (London, 1625); J. Kenyon, *The Civil Wars* (London: Weidenfeld & Nicolson, 1988), pp. 55–9.

English-style pot helmet with single sliding nasal bar, as worn by many cavalry troopers in the Civil War. (National Civil War Centre, Newark, with permission)

Troopers were usually armed with a heavy sword and often two pistols. They wore a buff leather coat on top of which they had back and breastplates and on their head they wore an open-faced pot helmet. It appears that contrary to the advice given in the earlier military manuals, carbines were usually only borne by the officers. Some men, usually but not exclusively officers, often brought their own personal armour and buff coats with them but the majority probably had theirs issued from the quartermaster. In the seventeenth century, apart from the dragoons who were actually mounted infantry, there were usually two types of cavalry used in most European armies; there were those who were described as 'heavily armoured' (cuirassier) and those described as 'lightly armoured' (arquebusier). The cuirassier was often slow and cumbersome and expensive to equip and required heavier horses to carry them and whilst there were a few at the start of the war, namely Essex's Lifeguard and Hesilrige's regiment, they were never widely recruited. The lighter arquebusier was well equipped for both the landscape of Britain and the swift movement across it to support both garrisons and field armies in times of conflict. By the end of the war this was by far the most popular form of cavalry in both Royalist and Parliamentarian forces. The activities of the Nottinghamshire horse under Francis Thornhagh suggests that they were certainly equipped as arquebusiers allowing them to be promptly deployed across the county, region and country to join up with similar regiments of horse under Colonels Oliver Cromwell and Edward Rossiter. It was Thornhagh's neglect to put on all his light armour at the battle of Preston in 1648, which left him vulnerable to receiving mortal

Arquebusier armour consisting of back and breast worn by troopers in the Nottinghamshire horse. (National Civil War Centre, Newark, with permission)

wounds from the Scottish lancers that rode out to meet him as he charged towards them.[6]

Francis Thornhagh began the task of raising a regiment for his father by persuading his friend and political associate Henry Ireton to return to Nottingham with what remained of his troop of horse and become his Major in the new regiment. To this group, according to Lucy Hutchinson, he also added '…many of the honest men that first enlisted themselves with Mr George Hutchinson became troopers'.[7]

By July 1643, the regiment had recruited and equipped at least four troops of horse for as Lucy Hutchinson again noted 'All the horse that had been raised in Nottinghamshire marched away with Sir John Meldrum, which [were] Colonel Thornhagh, Major Ireton, Captain White and Captain Farmer's troops'.[8]

Over the next three years, further troops of horse were also raised to serve in the regiment. The accounts of John Hough, treasurer of the Nottingham Committee, show that over the years 1645–1646 he had on his payroll six companies of foot and eleven troops of horse. The commanding officers of each troop were identified as Colonel Thornhagh, Lieutenant Colonel George Hutchinson, Major Meldrum, and Captains Charles White, Laurence Palmer, John White, William Hall, Thomas Selbie, Henry Champion, Barry Pendock and a Captain Barrett.[9] Any doubt as to the overall commander of these different troops had been resolved in September 1644 when George Hutchinson had gone to London and 'Procured a commission for Colonel Thornhagh to be, next under Sir Thomas Fairfax, commander-in-chief of all the Parliament's horse in Nottinghamshire at all times'.[10]

A further troop of horse under the command of Captain Dolphin has also been identified at Nottingham and shared garrison duties at Broxtowe Hall with some of Thornhagh's troops. It wasn't part of the Nottinghamshire horse under the command of Thornhagh though and was probably attached to the command of Colonel John Hutchinson at Nottingham castle to serve the garrison.[11] With command structures clearly in place, and a growing,

6 For more details about the cavalry see C. H. Firth, *Cromwell's Army* (London: Methuen & Co, University Paperbacks, 1962), Chapter 5 and Kenyon & Ohlmeyer, *Civil Wars*, pp. 234–6.

7 Keeble, *Lucy Hutchinson*, p. 99.

8 Keeble, *Lucy Hutchinson*, p. 114.

9 PRO, Accounts, of John Hough, SP 28/174 also Wood, *Nottinghamshire Civil War*, p. 135.

10 Keeble, *Lucy Hutchinson*, p. 174.

11 The Cromwell Association Online Directory of Parliamentarian Officers <https://www.british-history.ac.uk/no-series/cromwell-army-officers>, accessed 20 February 2019. A Captain Dolphin is also identified in the notebook of Lucy Hutchinson.

well equipped regiment ready to serve, though as with many other regiments often in arrears of pay, the Nottinghamshire horse went on to become a powerful mobile force both across the region and also the country.

In raising this regiment of horse, Francis Thornhagh incurred both a lot of personal debt and probably lent large sums of his own money. This becomes clear after his death in 1648. In October 1647, as a 'Member of this House' he submitted a petition for the reimbursement of £1,030, which he had spent 'in raising a Regiment of Horse for the service of this Parliament'. The Nottingham Committee also supported the petition. Parliament ordered that this sum should be raised out of the confiscated lands and rents of the deceased Nottinghamshire papist and delinquent Thomas Markham.[12] As late as August 1649, his widow was still petitioning Parliament for this sum of money, as it had proven difficult up until then to raise this sum out of the Markham estates. Along with this renewed petition an order issued by the Committee of the army had also been sent up via the Nottinghamshire MP Gilbert Millington requesting that a further £358.8s be paid to the widow. This was 'due to Colonel Thornhagh, for his Arrears since the time he came into the Establishment, to be paid to Elizabeth Thornhagh, his widow, out of the sequestrations of the Earl of Newcastle in the county of Nottingham'.[13]

Details of if, when, and how much of this money the family finally received have not survived. This might possibly explain some of the financial difficulties experienced by the Thornhagh estate over the 1650s and 1660s, which were only completely reversed when the son of Colonel Francis Thornhagh, John, came of age to run the estate after the death of his grandmother in 1662.

Military Activities of Colonel Thornhagh, 1643

Whilst garrisoned in and around Nottingham over the years 1643–1644, the most time-consuming military duty undertaken by the troops of Thornhagh's regiment would have been the supervision and collection of the weekly assessment levied on the Nottinghamshire villages. This assessment (the Royalist equivalent was known as contribution) was a levy imposed upon each village towards the cost of maintaining, equipping and provisioning the local garrison. Payments could be, and often were, made in either cash or goods with pease, hay, bedding and oats often making up the majority of goods. The parish constables would share out the sums levied across the whole parish and oversee its collection, and on a regular basis soldiers would visit both to collect the levies and by their presence encourage continued payment of the assessment. For the Nottinghamshire horse, each troop would have been allocated a number of villages from which it was responsible for collecting the assessment. Colonel Thornhagh would have had little, if any, involvement in these routine administrative duties, other than possibly adjudicating over friction between different troops around

12 HC Journal, V, 5 October 1647, p. 327.

13 HC Journal, VI, 17 August 1649, p. 280.

overlapping territories. In fact, Lucy Hutchinson implied that Thornhagh was far too lax in monitoring the actions of his troopers.

> During Colonel Thornhagh's sickness, the Governor [John Hutchinson] undertook the command of the horse regiment, whilst it quartered in the garrison and made them live orderly, and march out upon designs more frequently than they were used to when their colonel was well, upon whose easiness they prevailed to do what they list; and some of them who were great plunderers, were connived at, which the Governor would by no means suffer.[14]

A chance survival of accounts kept by Thomas Midlam for the outlying Parliamentarian garrison at Broxtowe Hall, which lay three miles to the north of Nottingham Castle, provide a brief glimpse into the actions of the troopers.[15] This outpost was garrisoned as part of a defensive circle around Nottingham in 1643, as Royalist forces were then in control of much of the county, with troops of horse under the commands of Captains, Charles White, Laurence Palmer and Richard Dolphin occupying it by rota. The earliest entries list beds, bedding and furniture being collected for the soldiers as the garrison was established. The assessments were collected from the constables of at least 16 villages and included loads of wheat, rye, oats and pease as well as cash. The troopers were not averse to using force, especially against individuals known to be in arms for the King: 'About ye 20th of November 1643 Itm seized and taken. Hay from Hucknall reputed to bee Sir John Byrons or Sir Richard Byrons by warrant from Captain Palmer dated ye 2nd of November 1643 to the number of aboute 20 loads priced £6.13s.4d'.[16]

At least the trooper's horses were well provisioned for the start of the winter months.

The accounts also record subsequent payments for goods taken by the troopers, possibly beyond their immediate remit. In November 1643, the treasurer recorded 'Itm rec'd one cowe of Mr George Flowers of Hucknall wch was killed for the maintenance of the souldiers at Broxtowe – paid £4'.[17]

Although each captain of horse in Thornhagh's regiment would have received from Parliament 'mounting money' of £1,100 to enable him to provide arms, horses and initial pay for his troopers, weapons and mounts were often lost both in minor skirmishes or major battles.[18] The accounts record such replacements in their pages 'Delivered to Thomas Robinson, one horse to bee ridden in the troope of the said captain [Laurence Palmer], which was lost in actual service – £5'.[19]

---

14 Keeble, *Lucy Hutchinson*, p. 168.

15 PRO, Parliamentarian Accounts for Broxtowe Hall, 1642,1646, SP 28/133, Part 2. Ff. 82–89. A transcript is provided in M. Bennett, S. Jennings, M. Whyld, 'Two Military Account Books for the Civil War in Nottinghamshire', *Transactions of the Thoroton Society (hereafter TTS)*, 100 (1996), pp. 107–21.

16 Bennett, Jennings, Whyld, 'Two Military Account Books', p. 111.

17 Bennett, Jennings, Whyld, 'Two Military Account Books', p. 111.

18 Firth, *Cromwell's Army*, p. 18.

19 Bennett, Jennings, Whyld, 'Two Military Account Books', p. 113.

Although collecting and accounting for the assessments probably occupied large parts of the routine of troopers over the years 1643–1644, for Colonel Francis Thornhagh obtaining additional cash from Parliament to reduce the arrears of pay for his men probably occupied much of his time and vexed him most. At the start of 1644, the treasurer at Broxtowe Hall recorded the arrival of cash from London via the town's MP who was still sitting at its meetings 'Rec'd of Gilbert Millington at London by order from Colonel Thornhagh – £50'.[20]

Although logistics and pay occupied a great deal of energy and time there were also periods of military activity over these years, two of which saw the regiment's commanding officer Colonel Francis Thornhagh seriously wounded. He was most certainly a senior officer not afraid to lead his men from the front and it is to these battles we now turn.

The first major military action that some of the troopers from the regiment were involved with, though surviving evidence suggests that their Colonel wasn't present, was the first siege of Newark (25–28 February 1643). According to Lucy Hutchinson a body of 700 men, including 200 from Derbyshire, left Nottingham to rendezvous with a force of one thousand horse, foot and dragoons from Lincolnshire under the command of Major General Thomas Ballard.[21] Their intention was to neutralise the fledging Royalist garrison of Newark before it became too well established. At first there appears to have been a degree of success to the north of the town where the Lincolnshire forces drove the Royalists from their defensive works and entered parts of the town. Ballard though, for reasons that still remain unclear, refused to back this initial success by sending his horse in as support and so the Royalists were able to rally. The next day Ballard refused to undertake a second attempt on the town and withdrew the Lincolnshire forces, leaving the Nottinghamshire and Derbyshire soldiers to the south of the town to make their own withdrawal. An early chance to take out the Newark garrison was therefore missed and this proved to be costly for the region over the next three years. According to Lucy Hutchinson, the senior officers of the Nottinghamshire contingent were Lieutenant Colonel John Hutchinson (foot) and Captain White (troop of horse).[22] The Nottinghamshire foot and horse behaved with competence and courage, but Hutchinson along with other senior officers reported Ballard to Parliament for his incompetence. The event also soured relationships between Hutchinson and Gell, with the former accusing Gell of withdrawing his Derbyshire forces and leaving the Nottinghamshire force to fend for its self.

By June 1643, Thornhagh's own troop and the whole regiment would have been fully operative and well equipped, though no evidence survives to ascertain whether either were at full strength. The horse had helped to establish a defensive garrison at Broxtowe Hall and would have been responsible for monitoring and, where possible, harassing the forces of Queen Henrietta Maria which had arrived at Newark on 16 June and numbered

20 Bennett, Jennings, Whyld, 'Two Military Account Books', p. 112.
21 Wood, *Nottinghamshire Civil War*, p. 39.
22 Keeble, *Lucy Hutchinson*, p. 104.

Seventeenth-century proto-mortuary sword, often used by officers in a calvary troop. (National Civil War Centre, Newark, with permission)

around 5,000 men. On 21 June around 2,000 of the queen's army appeared before Nottingham, seemingly to make an attempt of dislodging the garrison at the castle. A contemporary witness to subsequent events recorded 'The Parliament horse drew out of Nottingham to receive the Queen's [forces], but they came not on after the execution of the cannon … so when they saw they had lost their design, the horse returned again to Nottingham where the foot had stayed all the while they were out'.[23]

On this occasion Colonel Francis Thornhagh would have been at the head of the horse, encouraging them to prepare to meet the Royalist onslaught but for now it failed to materialise. This was to be remedied just over a month later at the battle of Gainsborough. As a result of this early attempt on Nottingham, Sir John Meldrum and the Nottingham committee appointed John Hutchinson as the Governor of Nottingham Castle, though his authority over the wider town was to become a focus for friction later.[24] The Queen and her forces finally left Nottinghamshire on 3 July to continue their journey to the King at Oxford.

The Battle of Gainsborough, 28 July 1643

The first major military action that involved both Colonel Thornhagh and troops from his regiment of horse was at the battle of Gainsborough in Lincolnshire. The town lay just seven miles away from the family estate at Fenton, but on the opposite bank of the River Trent. In April 1643, the Eastern Association had sent Oliver Cromwell and his regiment into Lincolnshire

23 Keeble, *Lucy Hutchinson*, p. 109.

24 Keeble, *Lucy Hutchinson*, p. 110.

to assist the Parliamentarian forces there. This additional support and strength encouraged the commander of the Lincolnshire forces, Lord Willoughby of Parham, to capture the town of Gainsborough and establish a garrison there to control the crossing of the River Trent. This Parliamentarian victory put increasing pressure on the Royalist garrison of Newark and potentially interrupted the communication links between Newcastle in the north and the King's headquarters at Oxford. In response, Newcastle began the journey southwards to retake the town and also ordered Lieutenant General Sir Charles Cavendish, commander of the Newark horse, to take as many troops as could be spared from Newark to begin besieging the town.[25]

Foxby Hill, Gainsborough. The incline has been reduced in constructing a road up it, but even so one still gets a sense of the steepness of the hill up which the Parliamentarian horse had to charge to confront the Royalist forces. (Author's photo)

On 25 July, Colonel Cromwell moved with 600 cavalry to lift the siege at Gainsborough. Meeting up with Sir John Meldrum at Grantham and Lincolnshire forces at north Scarle, 16 miles south of Gainsborough, he marched to confront Cavendish's forces outside Gainsborough on 28 July. According to Lucy Hutchinson 'All the horse that had been raised in Nottinghamshire marched away with Sir John Meldrum, which [were] Colonel Thornhagh, Major Ireton, Captain White and Captain Farmer's troop.'[26]

Cromwell wrote 'I marched after the taking of Burleigh House upon Wednesday to Grantham where I met about three hundred horse and dragoons from Nottingham; with these by agreement we met the Lincolners at North Scarle.'[27]

In total Meldrum's relief force, he was the General in command but is largely ignored by Cromwell in his subsequent reports, amounted to 22 troops of horse and three or four companies of dragoons possibly amounting to around 1,200 men.

The ensuing battle is believed to have taken place to the south east of the town. The Royalist forces were drawn up on the top of a steep hill, up which the Parliamentarians had to push forward. On the ascent they managed to repulse the first charge of the Royalist cavalry. The Nottinghamshire horse was right at the heart of this attack. The Lincolnshire forces, followed by Meldrum and the Nottinghamshire horse with Cromwell and his troops at the rear, led the advance up the hill. A second Royalist charge, led by Cavendish drove the front ranks of Lincolnshire and Nottinghamshire horse back but pushing his attack too far, Cromwell was able to regroup his troops and attack the Royalists

25 For more details of the battle of Gainsborough see Wood, *Nottinghamshire Civil War*, pp. 51–53.

26 Keeble, *Lucy Hutchinson*, p. 104.

27 C. H. Firth, *Memoirs of Colonel Hutchinson* (London: Routledge, 1906), p. 129. footnote 1.

in the rear. The Royalist troop were scattered towards Morton, with Lieutenant General Cavendish being killed in the pursuit. After the battle, Meldrum was able to get supplies into the Gainsborough garrison but then had to promptly make a well-organised strategic retreat back to Lincoln as the Earl of Newcastle with the whole of his Northern army arrived from Yorkshire.[28] Lucy Hutchinson recorded the following about the battle and its aftermath:

> Colonel Thornhagh, who had fought very gallantly; was taken prisoner, and after he was stripped of his arms and coat, a Major of the enemy's, whom the Colonel had lightly wounded in the fervour of the fight, came and basely wounded the Colonel, being disarmed, so that he left him for dead. But by he good providence of God, the wound which the enemy intended to give him death, gave him liberty; for coming to himself a little later after the hurt, he crept to one of his tenant's house, and there had his wounds bound up and found means to get to Lincoln.[29]

Lucy Hutchinson's account raises as many questions as it gives answers to about Colonel Thornhagh's exploits at Gainsborough. To a certain extent this is understandable as her *Memoirs* were focussed on honouring the exploits of her husband John and although Thornhagh was respected and much liked by both John and Lucy, notes about him were always an aside to the main narrative. We are not told when and how Thornhagh was captured, the most likely time probably being after the initial battle and during the subsequent retreat from Gainsborough at the appearance of Newcastle's army. According to one account of this episode, 'there was initially some disorder in the retirement of the cavalry, partly owing to the large number of hedges, which had to be negotiated.'[30] Half a mile further away from Gainsborough, Cromwell was able to rally the cavalry and a more orderly retreat, covered by Major Whalley and Captain Ayscoghe, took place. Captured during this initial period of disorder may well account for the action of the Royalist major 'whom the Colonel before had slightly wounded'. The officer and Thornhagh had met in the initial battle and the Royalist officer was probably able to rally to Newcastle's army on its appearance before Gainsborough.

Most, though not all, of the Thornhagh lands lay on the opposite bank of the River Trent in Nottinghamshire. This suggests that Colonel Thornhagh possibly got across the river – the area was well known to him from his youth – to find a safe place to recover amongst his tenants. This would make considerable sense, as the whole of Newcastle's army was encamped around Gainsborough for the next three days until the Parliamentarian garrison surrendered. Being on the other side of the river amongst those known to him was a safer option. His wounds, once dressed, could not have been too severe because he was able, according to Hutchinson, to get to Lincoln. This city was to be captured and garrisoned by the Royalists around 5 August. Thornhagh was certainly well enough to be able to travel the 10 miles and

28 P. Young and R. Holmes, *The English Civil War: A Military History of the Three Civil Wars, 1642–1651* (London: Eyre Methuen, 1974), pp. 151–3.

29 Keeble, *Lucy Hutchinson*, p. 114.

30 Young and Holmes, *English Civil War*, p. 153.

oversee the dispersal of what remained of his troops before the city's fall. At this time Thornhagh's Major, Henry Ireton, transferred with his troop to serve with the regiment of Colonel Cromwell, as return to Nottingham was not then possible.

With Newcastle's army established and in control across both north Lincolnshire and Nottinghamshire and the Royalist Newark horse resupplied and resurgent up to the outskirts of Nottingham itself, it wasn't possible for what remained of the Nottinghamshire horse or their Colonel to slip back into Nottingham for several weeks. Their whereabouts, and also that of Thornhagh himself over that period aren't recorded in the surviving records. They possibly either remained in and around southern Lincolnshire or relocated to Leicester. Captain White's troop didn't return to Nottingham, from Leicester, until around 26 September.[31] Being devoid of most of its horse over this period led the Parliamentarian committee for Nottingham to raise an additional troop of horse under the command of a local clergyman, Captain Laurence Palmer.

The battle of Gainsborough witnessed a reversal in fortune for the Nottinghamshire horse in addition to the wounding of their colonel Francis Thornhagh. The various troops were scattered and Major Ireton and his troop joining up with the regiment of Oliver Cromwell diminished the regiment further. Ireton went on to become the son-in-law to Cromwell after his marriage to his daughter Bridget in 1646. It wasn't until early September, after the Earl of Newcastle had removed his army back into Yorkshire, that Colonel Thornhagh 'before his troop was well raised … being recovered, brought back his troop from Lincoln [shire]'.[32] According to Lucy Hutchinson, the nature of Captain Palmer's appointment and questions about whom he was accountable to was to be a major point of friction for both Hutchinson and Thornhagh for several months to come.[33]

The Governor John Hutchinson, fearing an attempt on the town by the rejuvenated forces of Royalist Newark, quartered 'the horse in those lanes which were near to the castle'.[34] Hutchinson's caution proved justified for on 18 September, 600 Royalist soldiers under the command of Sir Richard Byron, were able to enter and occupy the town right up to the walls of the castle itself. Contrary to Colonel Hutchinson's commands most of his soldiers were sleeping in the town, leaving the Governor with just a handful of men and very few officers, to defend the besieged castle. A number of Hutchinson's soldiers, and possibly Thornhagh himself who may have been staying at his home in St Marys Hill a distance away from the castle, were able to slip out of the town when darkness descended and re-join the governor after the siege was lifted. Not until 23 September when Captain White accompanied by men from both the Leicester and Derby garrisons arrived at the town, were the Royalists driven out of Nottingham, though they remained in control of the fort at Trent Bridge until 13 October. At the end of this event, Lucy Hutchinson cursorily records that

31 Keeble, *Lucy Hutchinson*, p. 127.

32 Wood, *Nottinghamshire Civil War*, p. 56.

33 Keeble, *Lucy Hutchinson*, p. 123.

34 Keeble, *Lucy Hutchinson*, p. 124.

Colonel John Hutchinson, governor of Nottingham Castle and lifelong friend of Francis Thornhagh. Engraver V. Focillon. (Author's collection)

'Colonel Thornhagh having lost most of his troop, went to London to get another'.[35] This probably meant money, equipment and horses for new recruits rather than recruits themselves for over most of the first civil war the Nottinghamshire horse were clearly made up of predominantly local men who at times took some persuasion to move further afield.

Events Around the Turn of the Year 1643–1644

To a certain extent, events in Nottinghamshire from October through to January 1644 were shaped by the ebb and flow of the war in counties beyond its borders. Until the defeat of the Newark horse by the Earl of Manchester at Winceby in Lincolnshire on 11 October, the Royalists appeared to hold sway in the county even up to the town of Nottingham itself. Thereafter a brief interlude would have given Thornhagh and his junior officers a little time to enlist, train and accommodate his new troopers into the wider regiment. It was a brief interlude for Newcastle lifted his siege of Hull the day after Winceby and next month moved his army into Derbyshire before over-wintering in Nottingham.[36]

The main activities within Nottingham at this time appear to be focussed around consolidating the chain of command within the town. On 30 October, Hutchinson was raised to the rank of full colonel and on 20 November his governorship was extended beyond the castle and over the whole town, giving him military jurisdiction over both. This was supposed to clarify and limit the damage of fallout between Hutchinson and the town committee and also the various officers in the castle and town. Colonel Thornhagh, himself not immune from criticism by other officers, was surprised at this extension of the Governor's powers. According to Lucy Hutchinson:

> As soon as the Governor had received his commission … Colonel Thornhagh showed much discontent and was melancholy after it; whereupon the Governor told him that as he had not sought enlargement of command, so if any thought themselves abridged by it, or any other inconvenience to the public service, he would resign it and never make use of his commission. The Colonel answered him with much kindness that he only wondered how the town came to be added when they had only writ for the castle, but he was well satisfied with it.

35 Keeble, *Lucy Hutchinson*, p. 129.
36 Keeble, *Lucy Hutchinson*, p. 140.

The restored outer gatehouse at Nottingham Castle, through which Colonel Thornhagh led his troopers on foot to attack Royalist forces under Sir Charles Lucas. 16 January 1643/4. (Author's photo)

This disagreement was mentioned in the memoirs because it was unusual for the two close friends to have disagreements like this, which Lucy Hutchinson put down to envy rather than malice. They both 'were the most faithful and unbiased, and zealous champions of the public interest in their county'.[37] The new commissions did little to halt the disagreements between some of the committee and Hutchinson, as we shall see. They continued over much of 1644 and Colonel Thornhagh found himself and his command also challenged over this time. The year ended for Thornhagh on a more positive note when on 30 December 1643, Parliament appointed him to be the High Sheriff of Nottingham in place of the Royalist Sir John Digby. Because of the war, he was to retain this position until 1 December 1646 when 'Richard Hacker, Esquire' was appointed to succeed him to the position.[38]

The return of Newcastle, who had been created a Marquis in October 1643, and his army to Nottinghamshire at the start of December, created considerable consternation in Nottingham.[39] Hutchinson began extensive preparations at the castle for a siege, though the town still remained open. He sent all the Nottinghamshire horse, except for a few retained as scouts, to the adjacent county of Leicestershire. The horse would be of little use during a siege and would probably impact upon provisions. It is also likely that their commander,

37 Keeble, *Lucy Hutchinson*, pp. 138–9.

38 HC Journal, III, 30 December 1643, p. 354; HC Journal, Vol. 4, 1 December 1646, p. 733.

39 M. Bennett, *The English Civil War: A Historical Companion* (Stroud: Tempus, 2004), p. 175.

Colonel Thornhagh, went with them. Although parts of the Royalist force were quartered in the vicinity of the town, no siege was undertaken. The winter season was not the best time for soldiers to begin a siege and the Royalists had only just moved away from an earlier siege at Hull. Instead, an attempt was made to bribe Colonel Hutchinson to surrender the town, which he vehemently refused to do. Storm clouds were gathering in the north for Newcastle though, as the Scottish army began preparations to invade the north of England in support of Parliament (they crossed the River Tweed on 19 January 1644) and so in early January the northern Royalist army left Nottinghamshire to march towards the city of Newcastle to halt the Scottish forces.

Colonel Thornhagh and the horse arrived back in the town of Nottingham as soon as the Royalists had retreated, and was certainly back by 14 January. An attempt was made to move them on further north to support Sir Thomas Fairfax but they refused on two separate occasions the command to go even though ordered by Colonel Hutchinson. According to Lucy Hutchinson 'They made a sad confusing of powers, which the Governor [bore with] in respect to Colonel Thornhagh, who did things not so much out of malice as out of emulation, which did not destroy his kindness to the Governor'.[40]

It proved to be fortuitous that they stayed for on 16 January, 3,000 Royalists under the command of Sir Charles Lucas mounted a surprise attack on the town. They quickly occupied the town right up to the walls of the castle itself. Just as Lucas was about to summon the castle, the garrison there sallied out to confront the Royalists. The *Memoirs* give us few details of what happened but a letter written by Colonel Hutchinson after the event gives us much more detail:

> ... Colonel Thornhagh and all the other horse commanders encouraged their troopers to take muskets to their hands and serve as foot (which to their great glory they very cheerfully and courageously did) and with a foot company joined to part of them, sallied out and beat the cavaliers out of the nearest houses to the castle and possessed them.[41]

Seeing the success of this initial attack, two other companies of foot and the remaining troopers in the castle were sent out by Colonel Hutchinson to join the offensive and after much fierce fighting drove the Royalists out of the town. Again, as at Gainsborough, Thornhagh showed himself to be a very courageous commander, leading his soldiers from the front right into the heat of the battle. Once the Royalists were in full retreat to Newark, Lucy Hutchinson claimed her husband called his foot back to the castle, but ordered Colonel Thornhagh to pursue their defeated foe with the horse. There is no mention of such an order being disobeyed in any of Colonel Hutchinson's correspondence after the event. If an order had been given it was certainly not obeyed for no pursuit was undertaken. It possibly didn't occur because it was

40 Keeble, *Lucy Hutchinson*, p. 144.

41 Firth, *Memoirs of Colonel Hutchinson, Appendix XVIII*, p. 418. A small number of Colonel Hutchinson's surviving letters are to be found within the Tanner Manuscript Collection at the Bodleian Library, University of Oxford.

Early nineteenth-century print of Newark Castle and the old bridge over the River Trent. Engraver William Tombleson. (Author's collection)

getting dark and Thornhagh's troopers were exhausted after the day's action. Lucy Hutchinson was less gracious in her assessment of Thornhagh's motives in the *Memoirs* though, claiming it was because it was the Governor's idea and not his that he failed to act.[42]

The Second Siege of Newark (29 February–21 March 1644)

With Newcastle and his army occupied holding up the advance of the Scottish army into England and the Royalists of the region recovering from two military defeats at Winceby and Nottingham, the early months of the new year appeared to be a good opportunity for local Parliamentarian forces to neutralise the Royalist garrison at Newark. The Royalists had been further weakened by a number of its soldiers being removed from garrisons across the region and sent north under Sir Charles Lucas to support Newcastle in his fight against the Scots.[43]

In spite of this opportunity, it was end of February before local Parliamentarians were able to form a composite army to send against Newark. This consisted of men from Leicestershire, Lincolnshire, Nottinghamshire and Derbyshire. Although Lord Willoughby of Parham was present for part of the siege of Newark, command of the army overall was chiefly exercised by Sir John Meldrum. A series of prominent county commanders served under him at the siege, including Colonel Thornhagh who commanded the cavalry

42 Keeble, *Lucy Hutchinson*, pp. 147–8.

43 Martyn Bennett, *The English Civil War* (Hereford: Ditchfield, 1992), pp. 72–3.

Prince Rupert, the King's general of horse from 1642. (Author's collection)

contingent from Nottingham and Colonel John Hutchinson who commanded the Nottingham foot. A note in the Newark Borough minutes records that on 29 February Meldrum drew his forces in around the town and that the siege began.[44] The size of this besieging army has been estimated at between 5,000 to 8,000 men of which around 2,000 were cavalry.[45]

By early March, it was becoming obvious to Sir Richard Byron, Governor of Newark, that the town and garrison were in real danger of falling to the Parliamentarians and he sent out urgent appeals for help, both to nearby Royalist garrisons and also to the King at Oxford. Charles sent word to his nephew Prince Rupert, who was then at Chester, about the dire need of Newark claiming it could only hold out for a further 16 to 20 days. In response, Rupert set out from Chester on 12 March and moving through Chirk, Shrewsbury, Bridgnorth, Wolverhampton and Lichfield, which he reached on 17 March, he was able to add further soldiers from these garrisons to his army as it progressed. As he entered into Leicestershire, he was joined by a further 1,500 horse and 1,200 musketeers from Lord Loughborough at Ashby-de-la-Zouch and 1,000 horse and 600 musketeers under the command of Major General Porter.[46]

Although the Parliamentarians around Newark were aware of the possibility of Prince Rupert coming to break their siege, they had no information about his whereabouts and only sketchy information about the activities of local Royalist commanders. Early morning on 16 March Sir John Meldrum, disturbed by reports of growing military concentrations at Ashby-de-la-Zouch, sent Sir Edward Hartopp with 2,000 horse and dragoons from the siege to gather as much information as possible. It is not clear from the surviving evidence whether Meldrum intended Hartopp to try and thwart Major General Porter moving with his army from Tuxford to join up with Lord Loughborough's forces gathering at Ashby in anticipation of the arrival of Rupert, or just to reconnoitre local Royalist activity.

Details of what happened next are provided in a report submitted by Captain Lieutenant George Palmer to the parliamentary inquiry set up at Leicester following the defeat of their forces at Newark (see Appendix III).[47] Palmer was the officer appointed to take charge of Thornhagh's troop of horse whilst the Colonel remained at Newark with Meldrum. At the time

44 NA, Newark Borough Council Minutes, 1600–1662, DC/NW/3/1/1, 29 February 1644.

45 Wood, *Nottinghamshire Civil War*, p. 39.

46 For details of Rupert's march see Wood, *Nottinghamshire Civil War*, pp. 67–82.

47 'The Examination of Captain George Palmer taken before the Committee at Leicester, 30 March 1644', in E. W. Hensman, 'Mountsorrel' in A. Dryden (ed.), *Memorials of Old Leicestershire* (London: George Allen & Sons, 1911), pp. 126–7.

of the later inquiry, Thornhagh was still in a critical condition following his double wounding at the battle of Newark and there was still an element of doubt as to whether he would recover so it was Palmer that went before the inquiry instead of the regimental commanding officer.

By late morning on 16 March, Hartopp was in Leicestershire on the eastern bank of the River Soar at Mountsorrel.[48] A forlorn hope consisting of some troops from the Nottinghamshire horse under the command of Palmer, encountered scattered Royalist forces on the eastern side of the river and Palmer led his troop into an attack on the surprised enemy driving them back over the bridge where they ran into the body of a Royalist force. Hartopp refused to send further support to help Palmer and so the Royalist forces were able to regroup and counter attack splitting Palmers force into two, driving the Captain and part of the troop back over the bridge and leaving the rest trapped. These troops continued to fight bravely, though severely outnumbered. As the rest of Thornhagh's horse and others watched the events unfolding, anger began to rise at their colleagues desertion and contrary to orders, some of Thornhagh's horse along with some dragoons and Derbyshire horse under the command of Major Thomas Saunders fought their way back over the bridge to rescue their colleagues and bring them back to the main Parliamentarian force on the east bank. According to Palmer, the Nottinghamshire horse suffered a number of casualties and several were taken prisoner at this skirmish at Mountsorrel. Although Major Thomas Saunders was part of the Derbyshire force at this time he later went on to become the major in Colonel Thornhagh's regiment of horse and it may be that his actions in this skirmish were brought him to the attention of the Colonel after the event. Colonel Thornhagh was still rebuilding the command structure of his regiment following its defeat at the battle of Gainsborough and Saunders may have appeared to be an ideal candidate for the post.

Once Hartopp had got all of his forces back to the east bank, he began to move his army northwards towards Cotes Bridge. Here he intended to seize this strategic crossing in an attempt to stop Porter rendezvousing with Lord Loughborough's forces so as to significantly impede Prince Rupert's, still undetected, advance towards Newark. The land around the bridge, in fact there were two bridges connected by a causeway, was very marshy and prone to flooding and the bridge and causeway were the only way to get an army across the River Soar in this vicinity. On arriving at the village of Cotes on 17 March, Hartopp drew up his army to the east end of the village. Later that afternoon, he was joined by three companies of foot from Leicester under the command of Colonel Henry Gray who brought with them two cannons. The two small artillery pieces were to prove very effective in dislodging the Royalists from their defences on the western side of the bridge. According to Professor Bennett, the Royalist forces numbered between 1,500 to 2,000,

48 I am indebted to advice from Professor Martyn Bennett during discussions about the battle at Cotes Bridge. See also M. Bennett, 'The Civil War Battle at Cotes Bridge', *The Leicestershire Historian*, Vol. 3, No.3, (1984/5), pp. 15–21.

whilst Hartopp had a force of around 2,500 men.[49] In his account of events, Captain Palmer claimed:

> The next daye (17 March), being Saboath daye, some of the Nottingham troopes told Sr Edward in the Examrs hearinge yt if he would not suffer them to fight they would goe home, who answered that he had no commission to them to fight, and if their Collonell was there he would hange up some of them for being soe forward.[50]

Thornhagh and his officers had installed into the regiment a strong resolve to fight and even though he was absent that day, they were not afraid to express it. Whether, if he had been there, Thornhagh would have stood by and allowed Hartopp to hang some of his men is an interesting question. As it was, the events both at Cotes and Newark made the whole issue of subsequent military discipline immaterial. As a consequence of the troop's actions, Hartopp placed the Nottinghamshire horse two miles away from the fighting on top of Stanford Hill on the pretence of them looking out for the arrival of Major General Porter and his Royalist forces.

It was not until the morning of the next day (18 March) that Hartopp launched his attack on the bridge. With the support of the cannons the Parliamentarians drove the Royalist foot from their advance works on the bridge back to the Great Meadow and so secured both ends of the bridge and causeway. Throughout the rest of the day, the battle ebbed and flowed as the Royalist foot rallied but the Royalist horse had been driven back into the town of Loughborough. By the evening, the Parliamentarians had withdrawn back to the river to hold the bridge they had captured. Early the next morning on 19 March, Hartopp received word that Prince Rupert had arrived at Ashby and decided to withdraw his force back to Newark, via Stanford Hill to collect Thornhagh's regiment who had been there watching the fight below them. Arriving back at Newark, Hartopp was able to inform Meldrum of the developing situation and he may also have had a strong word with Thornhagh about the behaviour of his troops.

Although the Parliamentarian commander at Newark had been informed of Rupert's presence at Ashby by the return of Hartopp, by a mixture of stealth, speed and night time marches, the Prince was able to arrive on Beacon Hill, overlooking the town, by 9:00 am on Thursday 21 March, catching Meldrum by surprise. Rupert had with him the vanguard of his cavalry, with the foot arriving later in the day on its march from Bingham, just over 12 miles away. The details of the subsequent battle are somewhat shrouded by a mass of contradictory eye witness accounts, though it proved to be one of the bloodiest battles of the Civil War fought within Nottinghamshire, with around 300 slain from both sides. In many ways, picking through the details of this battle are beyond the immediate scope of this book and the reader is referred to other

---

49 Bennett, 'Battle at Cotes Bridge', p. 18.

50 PRO, State Papers Domestic, Charles I., Vol. 51, paper 56.

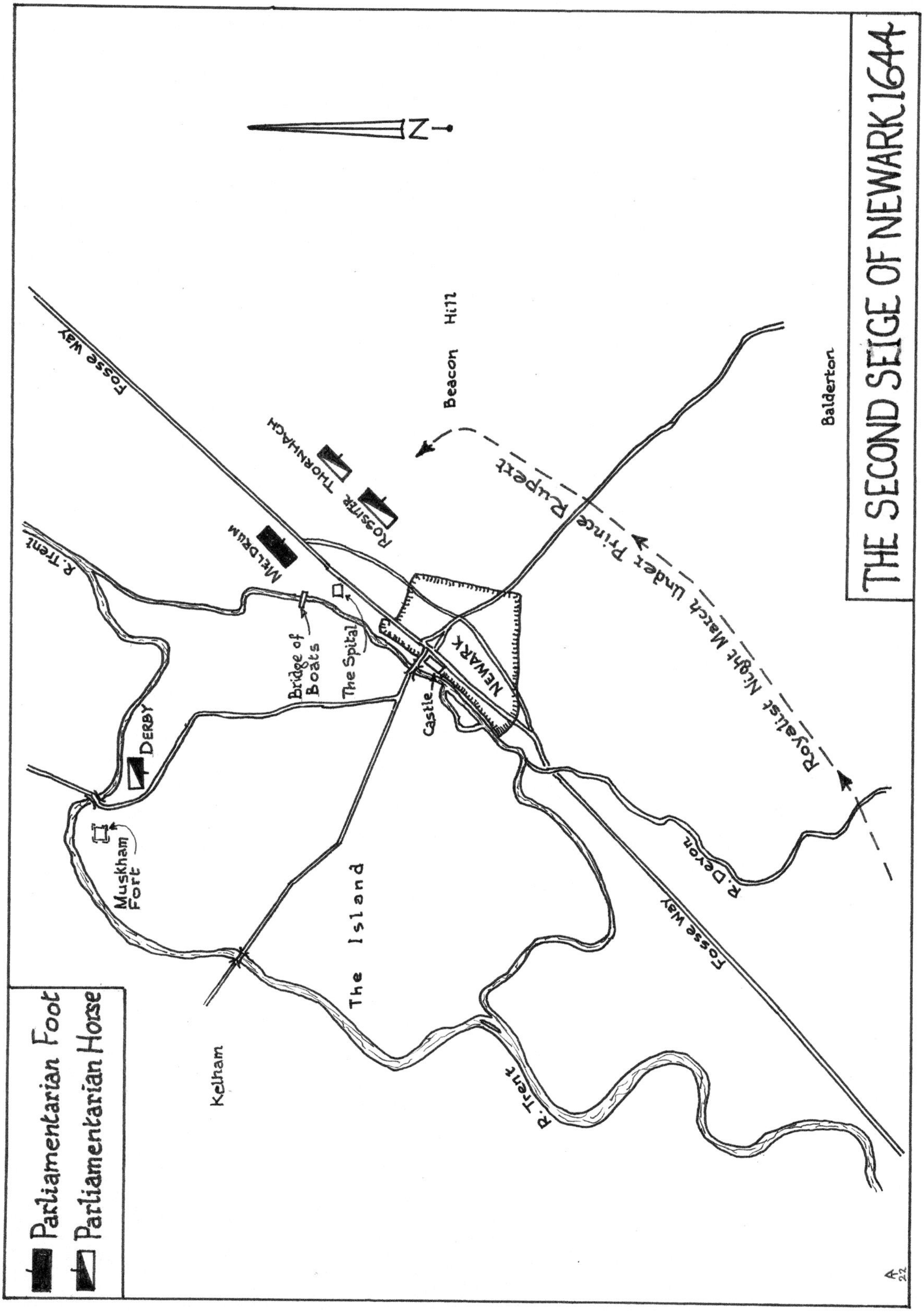
THE SECOND SEIGE OF NEWARK 1644
N
Parliamentarian Foot
Parliamentarian Horse
Fosse Way
Beacon Hill
Balderton
THORNHAGH
ROSSITER
MELDRUM
Royalist Night March Under Prince Rupert
NEWARK
Castle
The Spital
Bridge of Boats
DERBY
Muskham Fort
The Island
R. Trent
R. Devon
Fosse Way
Kelham
R. Trent

works for this discussion.[51] What follows will focus on the involvement of Colonel Thornhagh and the Nottinghamshire horse in the battle.

On arrival at the town, Rupert feared that Meldrum was preparing to retreat over the River Trent via a bridge of boats, to the island formed by two branches of the river and then cross over Muskham Bridge to make good his escape to Nottingham – in fact, Meldrum had already decided to stand and fight. Accordingly Rupert arranged his cavalry for a holding attack, till the rest of his foot caught up with him on its march from Bingham. Meldrum placed his army to the north of the town, around a ruined stone hospital known as the Spittal. He also sent some of his soldiers and horse across the river to the island to defend the fort and bridge at Muskham and cover his line of retreat if required. The bulk of his horse he sent to the foot of Beacon Hill to repulse any attack Rupert might make, placing Colonel Edward Rossiter in charge of the horse on the left and Colonel Francis Thornhagh commanding the Nottinghamshire horse and several troops of the Lincolnshire horse on the right wing. Thornhagh's regiment had been weakened at the battle of Cotes, so it was brought up to greater strength by these additional Lincolnshire troops. This time though, the regiment was going to be led from the front by its own Colonel. Both sides were about evenly matched in cavalry but surviving accounts differ as to who charged first.

As battle commenced, on the left Rossiter enjoyed some initial success, pushing the first line of Royalist attack back on to the second, but a subsequent charge by the reserve broke Rossiter's horse and drove them back in disarray to the Spittal. Thornhagh led the charge on the right wing and Lucy Hutchinson provided the following narrative of events that followed:

> But the Lincolnshire troops fled before even they charged, and left Colonel Thornhagh engaged, with only his horse, where, they say, he charged the Prince himself and made his way and passed very gallantly through the whole army, with a great deal of honour and two desperate wounds, one in the arm, the other in the belly.[52]

Thornhagh's bravery was also commented on in subsequent accounts of the action, where a Colonel Bury reported 'Colonel Thornhagh, a valiant gentleman, commanded that party which put the Prince to that distress'.[53]

The Parliamentarian horse were completely broken and Meldrum sent what was left of it over the bridge of boats to the island, leaving his foot dug in at the Spittal to face the rest of Rupert's army which had now arrived. At this time, a party of Royalists sallied out of the besieged Newark onto the island to capture the fort and bridge at Muskham. The remaining Parliamentarian horse on the island fled across the bridge and the small garrison of foot defending the fort quickly surrendered. There was now no escape for what

51 For further details alongside the account of Wood, *Nottinghamshire Civil War*, pp. 67–82. See also Bennett, *English Civil War,* pp. 70–9.; Young and Holmes, *English Civil War*, pp. 178–80.

52 Keeble, *Lucy Hutchinson*, pp. 156–7.

53 British Library, *Britaines Remembrancer*, 26 March–2 April (Thomason E40, 11) and also NA, *A Brief Relation of the siege of Newark by Colonel Bury* (1644).

Seventeenth-century pistol of a type possibly used by calvary troopers. (National Civil War Centre, Newark, with permission)

remained of Meldrum's army and with supplies running low, they negotiated for surrender. They were offered honourable terms by the Prince and marched away leaving behind in excess of 3,000 muskets, 11 cannons and two mortars, much-needed equipment for the local Royalist forces.[54]

This was a tremendous victory for both the Royalist cause and a personal triumph for Prince Rupert. Parliamentarians in the east Midlands were left very vulnerable and exposed, a situation not to be reversed until July when the Earl of Manchester with his army travelled south after the battle of Marston Moor (2 July). Although Prince Rupert had issued a summons to the garrison at Nottingham to surrender (25 March) he did not remain in the region long enough to force its surrender, being called by the King to return back to Oxford, two days after issuing the summons.

The defeat of the Parliamentarian forces in the region of Newark and the subsequent events would have been of little immediate concern to Colonel Thornhagh. He had been seriously wounded at the battle, with shots to his arm and stomach. He was brought back to Nottingham after the surrender in a wagon and the physicians there despaired of saving his life. Such wounds clearly demonstrate that this was a commander who was right at the heart of the battle with his troops. The wounds themselves raise some interesting questions though about how they were received, and more importantly how they were treated. The shot to Thornhagh's arm could easily have been received during the exchange of pistol fire during the initial melee as the two sides met each other in the charge. The stomach wound is slightly more problematic and medically more serious in an age before the availability of antibiotics. A musket ball fired by a pistol would not usually penetrate an arquebusier's breastplate. A shot fired from a more powerful musket or carbine, depending on angle and proximity of firing, often could. This might suggest that a Royalist officer, who would be armed with a carbine, or possibly a Royalist dragoon, shot Thornhagh in the stomach from close range. A dragoon was basically a mounted infantryman, whom Rupert would, on occasions, intersperse with his cavalry to provide additional cover for them. They would have had to dismount to fire their musket, as it was extremely difficult and dangerous to fire them whilst on horseback. Shot at from below

54 Young and Holmes, *English Civil War*, p. 179.

with a musket by a dismounted soldier, the bullet could actually go under the lower edge of his breastplate.[55]

Thornhagh would probably have been carried back to Nottingham with the musket balls still in his body. The garrison surgeon there would have at least two concerns that needed to be addressed almost immediately. The first would be the difficult task of locating and removing the shot which being of a soft lead would flatten on impact causing a wide cavity. Where possible, they were generally removed as left in the wound they could cause septicaemia as they underwent oxidation (rusting) over a period of time. Just as significant would have been the removal of foreign matter carried into the body by the shot. This might include cloth, metal splinters and dirt, which usually led to sepsis if neglected. Infection often killed as many soldiers as the shot itself. Once the musket ball had been removed and the wound cleaned a regular change of dressing was applied. This was usually linen soaked in either alcohol or turpentine mixed with other ingredients (each surgeon had their own preference), which kept the area sterile and malleable. The wound was usually kept open under the dressing to allow it to weep. According to Rutherford, modern medical practice (known today as 'delayed primary closure') has shown that this would have promoted 'the accumulation of lymph at the wound site, fortifying the immune system, recruiting white blood cells and limiting bacterial growth.[56] Although the modern scientific explanation and practice would not have been understood as such by seventeenth century surgeons, battlefield experience and recovery rates appear to have encouraged such practice. All of the above procedures would have been performed without any form of anaesthetic on Thornhagh, although he may have been allowed some alcohol to numb the pain before it began.

Undertaking this type of treatment would have been difficult just for the arm alone, but to perform it on a serious stomach wound would have been extremely dangerous. Thornhagh would have required treatment over an extended period of time and may well have experienced periods of fever, if any form of infection flared up. As far on as the late summer of 1644, Lucy Hutchinson was still referencing 'Colonel Thornhagh's sickness' during which period 'the Governor took command of the horse regiment'.[57] The Colonel was possibly nursed over this period in his own home at Nottingham, overseen by his wife and two young daughters, then aged three and one respectively.

55 Much of the above and what follows is derived from S. M. Rutherford, 'A new kind of surgery for a new kind of war: gunshot wounds and their treatment in the British Civil Wars' in D. J. Appleby and A. Hopper, *Battle-scarred: Mortality, medical care and military welfare in the British Civil Wars* (Manchester: Manchester University Press, 2018), pp. 57–77.

56 Rutherford, 'A New kind of Surgery', pp. 67–8.

57 Keeble, *Lucy Hutchinson*, p. 168.

Recovery and Duties to the End of the Year

Full physical recovery from the wounds he received at Newark took around four months and it is not until the end of the summer that Thornhagh's name begins to appear again in military and political orders and documents. Over the period of the summer, Colonel John Hutchinson exercised the command of Thornhagh's regiment. From his recovery bed in Nottingham, it would have been political rather than military matters that would have vexed Thornhagh most. The rift between the Governor of the castle and certain members of the town committee over issues of jurisdiction and command opened up again at this time with renewed angst. Even within Thornhagh's regiment there appears to have been some friction between the various officers about the chain of command. Hutchinson and members of the committee at Nottingham were summoned to London to present their cases and through Parliament find a resolution. On 4 October 1644, Lord Fairfax wrote from York to the Nottingham committee in support of Hutchinson's command. By the end of September, Thornhagh himself was well enough to make the long journey to London to speak before the authorities in defence of the actions of his old school friend John Hutchinson.[58] By the autumn a working resolution was arrived at, in which even Thornhagh's position was clarified. A new commission was issued to him which clearly stated that under Lord Fairfax he was to be 'commander-in-chief of all the Parliaments horse in Nottinghamshire at all times.'[59]

In August 1644, after the victory at Marston Moor, the Earl of Manchester marched south to help Parliamentarian commanders in the East Midlands take out a number of the remaining Royalist garrisons. These included the castles of Bolsover and Tickhill and the garrisons at Wingfield in Derbyshire and Welbeck, the latter being a home of the Marquis of Newcastle. According to the account of the Derbyshire Parliamentarian Colonel John Gell, Thornhagh sent his major and several troops of horse whilst Colonel John Hutchinson sent 200 foot from Nottingham to help in the taking of Wingfield, which surrendered on 21 August.[60] There may have been a number of factors which may have precluded Colonel Thornhagh from leading the horse to Wingsfield, but it is most likely that he was still not fully recovered enough to undertake military duties in the field at that time. Following the fall of Welbeck in north Nottinghamshire on 21 August 1644, Thornhagh was believed to be well enough to be appointed governor of the house, to which Newcastle had earlier sent his two daughters to live during the Civil War. Under Thornhagh they were permitted to remain at the house in peace, by direct command of the Lord Fairfax who later received a letter of thanks from them for their care.[61] Thornhagh was to be governor until Royalists under Major Jammot from Newark surprised the house on 16 July 1645,

58 A somewhat biased account of this disagreement is provided by Lucy Hutchinson in Keeble, *Lucy Hutchinson*, pp. 173-84.

59 Keeble, *Lucy Hutchinson*, p. 174.

60 Firth, *Memoirs of Colonel Hutchinson*, p. 200. footnote 1.

61 R. Bell (ed.), *Memorials of the Civil War* (London: Richard Bentley, 1849), Vol. I, pp. 194–195.

though the Governor was not present at the time of the attack. Thereafter it was de-garrisoned by mutual consent in November 1645.

During the winter months of 1644–1645, the Lincolnshire horse under Colonel Rossitor and the Nottinghamshire horse under Colonel Thornhagh watched Newark. Though closely monitored, the Newark horse continued to be a considerable threat to the whole of the region and Rossiter and Thornhagh had nowhere near enough troops to stem their raids from the town. A surviving account book for the regiment of Colonel William Staunton, a Royalist based at Newark, clearly shows that he was able to collect the contributions from villages for the garrison right up to within four miles of Nottingham from December 1644 right through to April 1645 when the accounts end.[62] On 7 December 1644 it was reported 'Colonel Thorney (sic) gave a great blow to a party of Sir John Girlington's horse at Muskham Bridge, whereof no doubt you have received intelligence before this time'.[63] Thornhagh captured officers, colours and horses in this daring raid. In December, Thornhagh marched against the fortified horse of Sir Roger Cooper at Thurgarton in Nottinghamshire. Supported by three companies of foot from Colonel John Hutchinson he stormed the neighbouring church and stables and compelled the defenders, about forty men, and Sir Roger Cooper to surrender.[64]

The Nottinghamshire horse and Colonel Thornhagh did not have it all their own way as they sought to tighten their grip upon Newark. The base of operations for the regiment over the winter appears to have been the town of Southwell, just less than seven miles away from Newark. Lucy Hutchinson records:

> The Nottinghamshire Horse, being in their own country, and having their families in and about Nottingham, were more guilty of straggling than any of the rest; and Capt. White's troop having presumed to be away one night when they should have been upon their guard, the Newarkers beat up our quarters, and took almost two whole troops of that regiment.[65]

In her notebook, Lucy Hutchinson recorded that the two troops were those of Captains Barrett and Sampson.[66] The Royalist newspaper *Mercurius Aulicus* reported the event on 6 January 1645 thus:

> Colonel Eyre went out with some Newark Horse, fetched a compass round about the rebels' headquarter, and broke down a bridge; then gallantly charged the rebels, who instantly fled towards the bridge, which being broken, made four of them drown themselves for haste; the rest, two whole troops, both officers and

62 Bennett, Jennings, Whyld, 'Two Military Account Books', pp. 116–21.

63 *The London Post*, 16, December 17, 1644 also referenced in Firth, *Memoirs of Colonel Hutchinson*, p. 217. footnote 2.

64 Keeble, *Lucy Hutchinson*, p. 190.

65 Keeble, *Lucy Hutchinson*, p. 191.

66 Firth, *Memoirs of Colonel Hutchinson*, p. 219. footnote 1.

> soldiers, were taken to a man, who, with their colours, horses, and arms, were brought prisoners to Newark.[67]

By the end of 1644, Parliament had begun to see some successes and for Nottinghamshire, the elimination of Newcastle's army at Marston Moor must have given both Colonels Thornhagh and Hutchinson some degree of comfort. Yet the war was far from won, and 1645 beckoned with new challenges for them both. For Thornhagh it would start with refurbishing the regiment following its losses at Southwell.

67 British Library, *Mercurius Aulicus,* 6 January 1645.

4

The Civil War: The Long Road to Victory, 1645–1646

Monitoring Newark: January to June 1645

Over the first six months of 1645, Colonel Thornhagh and the Nottinghamshire horse, alongside Colonel Rossiter and the Lincolnshire horse, continued with the task allocated to them by Parliament of restricting the activities of the Newark horse and, as far as possible, straiten the town of Newark. The Royalist garrison in the town had been strengthened over the last three months of 1644 and the two Parliamentarian colonels had far too few troops to either halt the raids or besiege the town. Their activities were generally limited to skirmishes and ambushes of Royalist troops as they foraged out across the surrounding parishes.

A more demanding task for Thornhagh over these early months was replacing the two troops of horse that had lost at the end of the year at Southwell. Finding decent horsemen to conscript into his cavalry regiment was one difficulty, but obtaining more weapons, armour, riding equipment and horses would have necessitated looking beyond Nottinghamshire, and possibly even the region, to be successful. The temporary resolution of the conflict between the Governor of Nottingham Castle and certain members of the town committee broke down again at the start of the year and rumbled on until April, providing another unfortunate distraction to Colonel Thornhagh and his military duties.[1]

Another more onerous and long-term appointment for Thornhagh was made by a Parliamentarian ordinance of 21 February 1645, when, along with others in the county, he was appointed to be one of several commissioners responsible for raising Nottinghamshire's contribution to the monthly pay of the Scottish army, which amounted to £31,000 per month. Nottinghamshire's contribution was to be £273.10s.5½d. per month.[2] In a county already stretched by levies and assessments towards the maintenance of two major

1 Keeble, *Lucy Hutchinson*, pp. 194–7.

2 C. H. Firth and R. S. Rait (eds), *Acts and Ordinances of the Interregnum, 1642–1660* (London: HMSO, 1911), Vol. 1, 21 February 1645, p. 642.

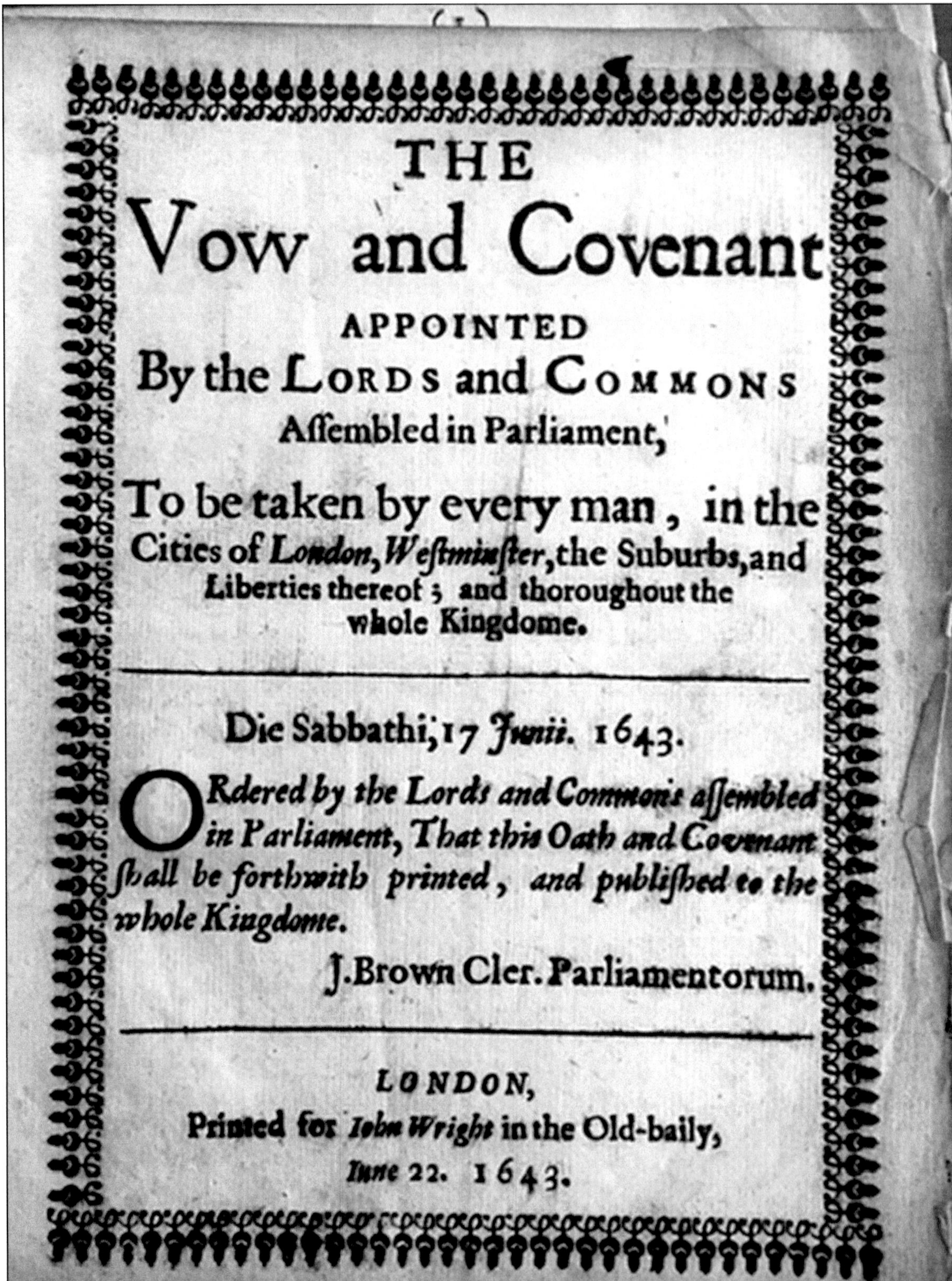

THE

Vow and Covenant

APPOINTED

By the LORDS and COMMONS

Aſſembled in Parliament,

To be taken by every man, in the Cities of *London*, *Weſtminſter*, the Suburbs, and Liberties thereof; and thoroughout the whole Kingdome.

Die Sabbathi, 17 *Junii*. 1643.

ORdered by the Lords and Commons aſſembled in Parliament, That this Oath and Covenant ſhall be forthwith printed, and publiſhed to the whole Kingdome.

J. Brown Cler. Parliamentorum.

LONDON,

Printed for *Iohn Wright* in the Old-baily,

Iune 22. 1643.

Facing page: The Solemn League and Covenant, an oath required to be sworn by all Parliamentarians as a consequence of the Scottish army marching into England in support of their cause against the King. Colonel Thornhagh retook the oath on being elected as an MP in 1646. (Author's collection)

garrisons, this additional payment proved to be extremely difficult to collect and it would fall upon some of Thornhagh's troops to undertake this. The situation was to get much worse for the county after November 1645 when the Scottish army arrived in the county to begin the third and final siege of Newark. The plundering and free quartering of the Scots across north Nottinghamshire, probably including the Thornhagh estate at Fenton, made this levy almost impossible to extract from many of the county's inhabitants. Colonel Thornhagh, who was also involved in the siege and had close contact with the Scottish army, was greatly aware of their impact upon the county and may well have been torn between his duty to Parliament and that of protecting the wider community of his own county.[3] Not until June 1646 was Thornhagh to find this additional responsibility removed from his shoulders.

Towards the end of February 1645, according to the Royalist newspaper *Mercurius Aulicus,* local Parliamentarian forces made an attempt to capture the moated house of Gervase Lee at Norwell. This attacking force consisted of around 200 foot from 'Lincoln, Welbeck and other adjacent garrisons and eight regiments [sic] of horse and one of dragoons'. By regiments the author probably meant troops of horse. Lying just less than nine miles to the north west of Newark, the Royalist had garrisoned it with 60 soldiers to serve as a satellite defensive garrison to the town. The morning after they arrived 'Colonel Thornhagh summoned the house, and being resolutely denied, made a hasty assault, but was so well beaten off by the gallant defenders that he left 28 men dead before the house, besides many wounded'.[4]

It would appear from the account that Colonel Thornhagh was the commanding officer and most of the troops of horse were probably from his own regiment and the dragoons were from the Nottingham garrison. This attack had to be halted promptly and a hasty retreat made to Retford on 25 February when Sir Marmaduke Langdale with 1,500 Royalist horse defeated Colonel Rossiter and the Lincolnshire horse at Melton Mowbray and moved on to rest at the garrison at Newark. Langdale had been sent by the King to relieve the besieged garrison at the castle at Pontefract. They remained briefly at Newark before moving on to their goal, but it was wisely decided by Thornhagh to abandon the siege at Norwell and await the return of a replenished Lincolnshire horse.[5]

Complaints continued to be sent up to Parliament about the activities of the 'Newark Horse' by parishes not only in Nottinghamshire but also across Lincolnshire and Derbyshire over the months March to May and it seems that Thornhagh was kept busy trying to monitor and intercept movements in and out of the garrison at Newark. They were forced to retire closer to Nottingham at the end of May when Charles and his Oxford army arrived at Ashby-de-la-Zouch on 27 May, for fear of an attempt being made on the town. In fact the King moved south, storming Leicester on 29 May and finally encountering the

3 S. B. Jennings, 'The Third and Final Siege of Newark (1645–1646) and the Impact of the Scottish Army upon Nottinghamshire and Adjacent Counties', *TTS,* Vol. 37:2 (Autumn 2012), pp. 142–62.

4 British Library, *Mercurius Aulicus,* 2–9 March 1645. See also C. Brown, *A History of Newark on Trent* (Newark: S. White, 1907), Vol.2, p. 79.

5 Wood, *Nottinghamshire Civil War,* pp. 88–9.

New Model army under the command of Lord Fairfax at Naseby on 14 June 1645. Here the Royalists experienced a devastating defeat, with the King losing nearly all his foot and his horse being considerably diminished, though a number, including Rupert's and over 400 Newark horse, did manage to escape the battlefield successfully. Through all of this Thornhagh and his regiment were instructed to remain and continue to monitor the comings and goings at Newark, and therefore were not involved at all in the Naseby campaign.

The Field Army of the Northern Association

On 20 June 1645, Parliament reissued an ordinance 'for associating the counties of York, Lancaster, Nottingham, Bishopric of Durham, Northumberland, Cumberland and Westmoreland into a Northern Association and for the raising of monthly assessments therein', to pay for that army.[6] Sydenham Poyntz was appointed commander-in-chief of all the forces of this association, with the rank of colonel general and on 19 August made Governor of York also.[7] According to the ordinance, this field army was to consist of 2,600 horse, 400 dragoons and 7,000 foot. The county of Nottinghamshire were to supply 'three hundred and twenty four horse … [and] eight hundred and two foot'. How many of these numbers Nottinghamshire was able to supply is unclear, but in effect from August onwards, Colonel Thornhagh and his regiment of horse became part of the Northern Association's cavalry with Colonel General Poyntz becoming Thornhagh's commanding officer.

A twentieth-century historian wrote that the defeat of the Royalists at Naseby made 'the flame of war burn all the brighter' for Newark and Nottinghamshire.[8] Following the surrender of a number of Royalist garrisons across the north, including Scarborough and Carlisle, the stronghold of Newark proved to be a rallying point for those supporters of the King who sought to continue the fight. With this new influx of forces, the Royalists undertook a number of raids across the region including the re-taking of Welbeck on 16 July and the destruction of Torksey House and capture of its garrison on 1 August 1645. Over the ten weeks following Naseby, Colonel Thornhagh and the Nottinghamshire horse were kept busy trying to contain the Royalists at Newark as Poyntz with parts of the Northern Association continued to subdue the remaining Royalist centres across the north.

The King, with what remained of his forces across the region, decided to try and join up with the forces of the victorious Earl of Montrose in Scotland and combine their forces against Parliament. He made a brief stop at Welbeck on his journey on 15 August, but finding his way north blocked by Poyntz and with the Scottish army and the Lincolnshire horse following him from the south, Charles reluctantly returned to Newark on 21 August. The

6 Firth and Rait, *Acts and Ordinances of the Interregnum,* Vol. 1, 20 June 1645, pp. 703–14.

7 D. N. Farr, 'Sydenham Poyntz' in the *Oxford Dictionary of National Biography* (hereafter *ODNB*) (Oxford: Oxford University Press, 2004), vol. 45, pp. 200–1.

8 Wood, *Nottinghamshire Civil War*, p. 94.

next day, to avoid being caught by these forces, he moved south towards his headquarters at Oxford. Parliament ordered Poyntz with his Northern Association forces to follow the King. He arrived at Nottingham not long after Charles had left Newark but at the town part of his army refused to move any further without some of their back pay being met. It took a couple of days to resolve the mutiny, but the Yorkshire horse still refused to go with him and returned back to their homes. In their place Poyntz took the Nottinghamshire horse and Thornhagh with him. As the army moved after the King, Colonel Thornhagh was sent to London to report at length the situation to Parliament and was to catch up with his regiment as the forces of Poyntz followed the King into Wales.[9]

Colonel General Sydenham Poyntz, appointed commander of the Northern Association in June 1645. The Nottinghamshire horse and their colonel, Francis Thornhagh, were placed under his command, (Author's collection)

The journal for the House of Commons records both Thornhagh's presence and its response to his report and actions in the entry for 30 August 1645:

> The house being informed that Colonel Thornhagh was at the door, sent hither from Colonel Poyntz. He was called in; and did acquaint the House with the state of the Forces in the Northern Counties, both English and Scottish, the mutinying of the Yorkshire Horse, and the occasions and grounds of it as it most probably appeared. Resolved & c. that two very good and serviceable Horses shall be forwith provided, and bestowed by this House upon Colonel Thornhagh, as a mark of his [sic] Esteem they set upon his many and good services performed to this great Cause maintained by the Parliament: And that it be referred to Sir Philip Stapilton and Sir Arthur Hasilrig to take care of the providing these horses. And that it be forthwith paid for, by the Committee of Lords and Commons for Advancements of Monies, at Haberdashers Hall. The care whereof is more particularly referred to Mr Hill.[10]

Thornhagh, after the debate, was called back into the chamber to be personally thanked by the speaker on behalf of the House. The fact that two of the House members were appointed to make sure that the horses were actually provided and funded provided via a named individual at Haberdashers Hall strongly suggests that the horses were actually presented to Colonel Thornhagh. He was probably able to use them in relay, to rejoin his regiment with greater speed who were then on the march with Poyntz.

9 Wood, *Nottinghamshire Civil War*, pp. 95–97.
10 HC Journal, IV, 30 August 1645, p. 258.

Whilst the King was at Chirk Castle in Wales, he received a message from Lord Byron at Chester stating that the city was besieged by Parliamentarian forces and required immediate assistance if it was to survive. Being only 20 miles away from the city, Charles decided to respond immediately, being at this time unaware of the close proximity of Poyntz's forces to him. Here outside Chester the two armies were to meet in a fierce cavalry battle on Rowton Heath.

The Battle of Rowton Heath (24 September 1645)

The city of Chester lies on the English east bank side of the River Dee. On 19 September 1645, Cheshire Parliamentarians surprised the Royalist garrison at Chester with a force of 500 horse, 200 dragoons and 700 foot. They rapidly besieged the city on the English side of the river and after intense fighting were able to take some of the suburbs, forcing the Royalist defenders to retreat behind the city's ancient walls. Yet in spite of this success, the Parliamentarians failed to secure the west, or Welsh, bank of the river and on the evening of 23 September after a rapid match, the King was able to approach the Dee Bridge. Charles divided his forces, taking with him into Chester, a small number of infantry, his Lifeguard and Lord Charles Gerard's horse, amounting to between 600–800 men, to boost the ranks of the city's defenders.

The majority of the Royalist horse, under the command of Sir Marmaduke Langdale, and amounting to around 3,000 troopers were sent eight miles south to cross the river at Holt on a bridge of boats. The intention was for this force to surprise the besiegers by circling around them and attacking from the rear. Unfortunately for the Royalists, they did not discover the presence of a second Parliamentarian force under Poyntz, until the evening of 24 September when a scout conveying messages between the two Parliamentarian forces was captured. Langdale responded quickly and at 9:00 a.m. on 25 September he charged the army of Poyntz and drove them back with considerable success, though he failed to rout the force completely, which allowed them to regroup later. Langdale returned to Rowton Heath to take up a more defensive position and sent word to the King in Chester asking for reinforcements. At the same time Poyntz sent a request for help to Colonel Michael Jones who was besieging the city. It was the Parliamentarians who responded first and a series of cavalry skirmishes followed, with the Royalist forces taking heavy casualties from the musket fire of Jones dragoons and foot. The Royalist relief force, under the command of Gerard had a hard fight getting through the suburbs to go to the relief of Langdale on Rowton heath, but on arrival had a degree of success against the Parliamentarian forces. At this point of the battle, Colonel Thornhagh and the Nottinghamshire horse come on to the centre stage of unfolding events.[11]

The Parliamentarian newspaper *Perfect Occurrences* printed the following report of these events on 9 October 1645:

11 John Barratt, *The Great Siege of Chester* (Stroud: Tempus, 2009), pp. 81–106.

We have been indebted to the Nottingham Horse for their good service in the last routing of the King near Chester, as you may see by Colonel Thornhagh's letter:

Sir – in pursuit of the King so far I pursued, that retreat I could not, fight I must commending myself and soldiers to God's protection, I resolved to charge them with my regiment. The enemy came on to us, and in a career charged; we stood and moved not till they had fired, which made Gerard swear (God damn him) "the rogues will not stir". Upon these words we clapped spurs to our horses, and gave him such a charge as I dare say was the accomplishment of the victory, for we routed him and pursued him, which made him fly to Holt castle, over a river in the night, with six men of a thousand which before were with him.

Francis Thornhagh
September 30[12]

King Charles Tower on the walls of Chester. Tradition claims that the King watched the defeat of his forces on Rowton Heath from this tower. (Author's photo)

In this letter we discern not only the voice of Thornhagh but also something of the young Colonel's character. A man of devout faith, he begins the fight with a brief prayer commending both himself and his men to God. He courageously stands firm with his men when under fire and with a degree of military expertise knows exactly when to launch the countercharge, which will break his opponent. In his willingness to lead the countercharge, we see something of the impetuousness that had contributed to him being wounded previously and were to have fatal consequences only two years later.

In November 1645, the House of Commons acknowledged the important contribution of the Nottinghamshire horse in this victory by issuing an ordinance 'For the payment of one thousand pounds, in course, with interest of the same, out of the Receipts of the Excise, to be paid to Colonel Thornhagh, or Gilbert Millington [the town's sitting MP], Esquires for the service of the horse at Nottingham'.[13]

Following the defeat of his army, and not wanting to find himself trapped in Chester, the King rode out of the town with 500 horse on 25 September into North Wales. Rendezvousing around Holt Castle, over the next couple of days he managed to rally 2,400 horse, but his army was now a shell of its former self. The garrison at Chester though proved to be more resilient then the Parliamentarians expected and under Byron's command it was to hold

12 British Library, *Perfect Occurrences*, 9 October 1645. See also Firth, *Memoirs of Colonel Hutchinson*, p. 230. footnote 3.
13 HC Journal, IV, 10 November 1645, p. 337.

out to 3 February 1646 before surrendering.[14] Poyntz, along with Thornhagh and the Nottinghamshire horse, took a few days to rest and reorganise their soldiers following the battle outside Chester. On 28 September, the Northern Association army moved across into north Wales in pursuit of the King and proceeded to track him and his small force all the way back to Newark.[15] Charles arrived at Newark on 4 October and was to remain there until forced to flee on 3 November. The Royalist forces were quartered around Belvoir, Wiverton, Shelford, Welbeck and across the county to try and reduce the strain on the town of Newark. Once Poyntz arrived at Nottingham he could use the Nottinghamshire horse, with their local knowledge, to harass the King's forces in their various quarters. A party of 20 Nottinghamshire horse surprised and routed around 50 of the Queen's regiment quartered at East Bridgford whilst troopers from Thornhagh's regiment were also involved in a successful skirmish with Royalists quartered at Langar.[16]

The Newark garrison certainly needed to be contained. Over the late summer, whilst Thornhagh and the Nottinghamshire horse were with Poyntz trailing the King, the Royalists had caused considerable disruption across north Nottinghamshire raiding the various parishes to requisition food and goods to stock up their garrison for the long winter ahead. Even the Thornhagh estate at Fenton appears to have been targeted over this period. Over the first three years of the war, Lady Jane Thornhagh, the widowed mother of the Colonel, remained at the family home, which had been granted to her as a dower. The constant harassment of soldiers from Newark over this period led to her to petition parliament for help. On 20 September the Commons journal recorded 'That the humble Petition of the Lady Thornehagh, widow be referred to the Committee at Haberdashers-Hall, to accommodate her with a House and Furniture, according to the desire of her Petition'.[17]

There survives no record as to what, if any, house the committee at Haberdashers' allocated to her. The return of Poyntz to Nottinghamshire and the record of a funeral cortège setting out from Fenton Hall in November (see Chapter 1) all suggest that her absence was to be a short one, if it happened at all.

The constant arrival of petitions from Nottinghamshire and surrounding counties persuaded Parliament to make the neutralising of the troublesome Newark garrison a top priority. Using the forces of the Northern Association and the services of the Scottish army, along with other soldiers from across the region, plans were put into place to make it happen.

The Third and Final Siege of Newark, 1645–1646

Although Poyntz had received instructions to try and block up Newark, possibly with the King in it, he had neither the troops nor resources to begin

14 Barratt, *Great Siege of Chester*, p. 164.
15 Barratt, *Great Siege of Chester*, pp. 111–2.
16 Wood, *Nottinghamshire Civil War*, p. 97.
17 HC Journal, IV, 28 September 1645, p. 281.

a close siege of the town. The situation was made even more difficult by the withdrawal of the Yorkshire horse, which returned back to their own county. On 4 November the London committee wrote to the York committee complaining of their removal, stating that 'for want of your forces, Col. Poyntz is forced to return to Nottingham'.[18] During this period of preparation and the taking out the smaller satellite Royalist garrisons encircling Newark, the King managed to slip out of Newark on 3 November with a bodyguard of around 500 horse, thus avoiding becoming trapped, and made his way back to his headquarters at Oxford.

Poyntz, Thornhagh and Rossiter were far from inactive over the months of October and November 1645. Thornhagh in particular appears to have been very busy securing information about the activities of Newark Royalists and the plans of the King. On 6 October Thornhagh and Captain White sent a deposition from Nottingham to Parliament expressing fears that the war might be extended by Royalist subterfuge with the Scots. They wrote:

> George Biggin, of Eakin [Eakring] informeth Mr Hawden, of Tuxford, minister, that a Trumpet belonging to Col. Eyre, of Newark, passed through Tuxford on Sunday, the 5th of this instant October, did in the presence of the said Mr Hawden, say and affirm that he was going with letters from his Majesty and from Sir Richard Willis, Governor of Newark, to General Leven, with hopes to bring him back with his army to Newark for the King, with as much joy as ever he did come for the Parliament: and Mr Hawden did see the two letters in the hand of the Trumpeter. And two Scottish gentleman being at Tuxford with Mr Hawden the same day, he did affirm to them that the King and General Leven had long been in treaty, and he did not doubt but it was affected, and that this letter would bring him back. Taken at Nottingham in the presence of us
>
> Oct: 6, 1645
> Fra: Thornhagh
> Charles White[19]

Alongside commanding his regiment of horse, it would appear that Colonel Thornhagh had in his employment a network of spies and observers around, and possibly even inside of Newark watching the comings and goings into the town.

The long awaited arrival of the Scottish army before Newark, to support the Parliamentarian forces, had been considerably delayed because they were poorly equipped and in considerable arrears of pay. This was because money promised to them by the English Parliament had not been forthcoming. Their commander was in no position to be able to move them without an advance of some money. It wasn't until 26 November 1645, that they finally appeared to the west of the town to begin the siege. Even then, they arrived in a pitiful state and clothes, weapons, shoes and ammunition had to be sent from

18 C. Brown, *A History of Newark-on-Trent* (Nottingham: Nottinghamshire County Council, 1995), 2 volumes, II, p. 91.

19 Brown, *History of Newark,* II, p. 94.

Newark Castle curtain wall viewed from the island formed by the River Trent dividing into two branches. The Scottish forces quickly secured this island at the start of the third siege. (Author's photo)

London to fully equip the army.[20] The Scots had originally been promised by Parliament a monthly sum of £21,000 but local commissioners across the country appointed to raise this levy from within their counties found it extremely difficult to raise any additional money from an already over-assessed population. On 21 February 1645, an ordinance had been passed appointing commissioners to raise this sum and Colonel Thornhagh was one of those appointed for Nottinghamshire to raise the allocated monthly sum of £273.10s.5 1/2d. From first-hand experience he would have been aware both of the difficulty of raising this money but also the effects of no pay and poor provisions had upon soldiers. He possibly therefore had mixed feelings about the growing delay in the arrival of this help.[21]

By the end of October 1645, realising that a close siege was not immediately possible, Poyntz and the local Parliamentarian commanders made the decision to 'take out' the satellite garrisons around Newark. It was deemed too dangerous to leave them to possibly launch attacks upon their forces from the rear once a siege could be begun. The first of those garrisons to be targeted was the manor house at Shelford, which the defenders had fortified with a strong palisade with a wide and deep ditch, or moat, below it. Its governor was Colonel Philip Stanhope, a son of Lord Chesterfield and his garrison consisted of around 200 men, including the remnants of the Queen's regiment. Colonel General Poyntz left Nottingham with both

20 Jennings, 'Third and Final Siege of Newark', pp. 142–62.

21 Firth and Rait, *Acts and Ordinances, I*, pp. 642., 21 February 1645.

infantry and some cavalry and rendezvoused with Colonel Rossiter and the Lincolnshire horse just outside the village of Shelford, which they intended to make their base for the siege. According to Lucy Hutchinson, a few Royalist soldiers had shut themselves up in the church tower and were shooting at the Parliamentarians as they entered the village forcing Colonel Hutchinson to smoke them down from the steeple. This would have caused considerable smoke damage to the interior of the church. The Governor of Shelford was offered generous terms of surrender, but these he flatly refused to accept. The storming of the house was planned for 3 November and as surrender had been refused, and the outworks had been so ferociously defended, Poyntz gave the order that no quarter should be given to the defenders.

Both Thornhagh and the Nottinghamshire horse were present at Shelford, as also were the Lincolnshire horse, but neither appeared to have taken part in the storming of the house. This was not unusual as both sides over the course of the war had preferred to use infantry rather than the more mobile and better-trained cavalry for such actions. Poyntz also feared an attempt by the Newark garrison to come to the aid of Stanhope and so he kept the horse in reserve ready to intercept any such relief force. In a passage that Lucy Hutchinson wrote to disparage Captain White whilst praising her husband, the absence of the horse from the storming is clearly implied.

> Captain White came to him [Hutchinson] and, not withstanding all his former malicious prosecutions, now pretends the most tender care and love that could be declared, with all imaginable flattery; and so persuaded the Governor not to hazard his own person in so dangerous an attempt, to consider his wife and children, and stand by among the horse, but by no means to storm the place in his own person.[22]

Hutchinson paid no heed to White's suggestion and led the Nottingham foot alongside a London regiment in storming the defended house. The fight was short but extremely bloody with 140 of the defenders being put to the sword and its governor fatally wounded. According to Lucy Hutchinson, it was her husband who found the stripped and dying Colonel Stanhope in the house, and covered him with his cloak and arranged for him to be carried to his own quarters for a surgeon to attend to him. It was to no avail as his wounds were too severe and he died that evening.[23]

Within 48 hours of taking Shelford, Poyntz drew up his army in front of the garrison at Wiverton and again issued a summons for its surrender. News had reached the Royalist defenders there of what had happened at Shelford, and Newark's failure to come to their aid, and they surrendered immediately on what were favourable terms without a shot being fired. From here Poyntz and Rossiter moved on to the Royalist garrison at Belvoir, making their headquarters at Bottesford. Hutchinson and Thornhagh were not at Belvoir and it appears most likely, given their local knowledge, that they

22 Keeble, *Lucy Hutchinson*, p. 202.
23 Keeble, *Lucy Hutchinson*, pp. 203–4.

were sent on to Newark both to monitor the garrison and also to begin to create some of the defensive works to the south and east of the town and the River Trent in anticipation of the siege. An attempt at storming the outworks of Belvoir proved extremely costly to Poyntz's forces and so a decision was taken to blockade the garrison instead. At the end of November he left six troops of horse and 500 foot to do this and marched to Newark to join the Nottinghamshire forces and the Scottish army, which by then had arrived.[24]

Although the Scottish army had quickly secured the island in front of Newark, formed by the two branches of the River Trent, the circumvallation to the west and south of the town was not completely secured until around the end of February 1646. This not only reflected the difficulty of constructing siege works but also the fact that Poyntz was still short of men and was awaiting further troops from the Eastern Association, Northamptonshire and Leicestershire. The Scots were more fortunate in that they had the river as their first line of defence and were quickly able to build sconces on the island and by Muskham Bridge, which crossed over the other branch of the Trent. The Nottinghamshire Parliamentarian forces, both horse and foot, appear to have been incorporated into Poyntz's Lifeguard and were based at the fort at Farndon with Thornhagh's horse being a little further back at East Stoke. A Parliamentarian newspaper dated 9–16 January 1646 noted:

> The Nottingham forces do keep their court in the church [east Stoke] where unfortunately happened so great a fire, which took hold of the straw, that they could not quench it until it had devoured all that was combustible by the fire, and nothing on the next morning but the walls remaining, a sad spectacle to the beholders.[25]

It appears that there was more than just hay to sleep on in the church, and the loss of both equipment and fodder would have hit the Nottinghamshire forces considerably hard in the midst of a severe and very cold winter.

A shortage of soldiers, coupled with the ongoing task of completing the lines of circumvallation meant that for the first three months of the siege the Royalists in Newark were able to sally out and attack both the Parliamentarian and Scottish troops on the siege works and they were even able on occasions to bring in more provisions. There would have been numerous skirmishes and fights but details of only a few of these were noted in the surviving records. The *Perfect Diurnell* records one such event on 10 December 1645 when a group of Newark Royalists sallied out at Farndon. One of the Royalist officers in the raiding party 'in a bravado flourished as if he would challenge any man to fight with him'. The impetuous Colonel Thornhagh rode out to take up the challenge and in a single charge dismounted the Newarker, killed his horse and took him prisoner. On the return to his own line, the watching Parliamentarian troops, including his own regiment, greeted him with cheering and much applause.[26] Whether this account was just propaganda

24 Wood, *Nottinghamshire Civil War*, pp. 105–6.

25 Brown, *History of Newark*, II, p. 99.

26 British Library, *Perfect Diurnell*, 8–15 December and 12–22 December 1645.

or an actual event is unclear, but it is certainly in keeping with the character of Thornhagh that we have encountered elsewhere. The troops may have enjoyed the spectacle, but his commanding officer, Colonel General Poyntz, would have been far from impressed by the recklessness of one of his senior officers and words may have been exchanged on his return.

At the end of December, 300 Royalists from Newark rode out and attacked the quarters of Rossiter's Lincolnshire horse on the siege lines causing considerable mayhem before finally being driven back into the town. An even greater raid occurred in January 1646 when 800 horse and 300 foot attacked the Parliamentarian commanders headquarters at Farndon, where both Poyntz's Lifeguard and Thornhagh's horse were quartered. Poyntz was nearly captured, being forced to defend himself with his sword. It is more than just a possibility that Thornhagh himself was caught up in this fight. The Royalist returned to Newark claiming they had taken over a 100 prisoners and killed many other soldiers.[27] This was probably the last major skirmish before the siege works surrounding the town were completed.

The defence works were completed with considerable haste after the January fight. The surrender of the Royalist garrison at Belvoir castle on 31 January, released those troops left to blockade the place, and they were able to rejoin Poyntz at Newark. The arrival of additional troops and a mortar from the Eastern Association around the same time meant that by the end of February the siege was secure and raids from Newark considerably reduced if not altogether halted.

The End of the First Civil War

Colonel Thornhagh and the regiment of Nottinghamshire horse were to remain at the siege of Newark for six months, until its surrender on 6 May 1646. It many ways the ending of the siege was bound up with the ending of the war nationwide. The surrender of Newark most certainly brought to an end the fighting within Thornhagh's home county of Nottinghamshire.

Across the country, February 1646 proved to be point at which the Royalist cause imploded. On 16 February the remnants of the Royalist army in the west, under the command of Lord Hopton, was defeated at the battle of Torrington. In that same month, the last Royalist port at Chester, where Thornhagh had fought with distinction, finally succumbed to the Parliamentarian siege and surrendered on terms. The last Royalist force in the Midlands under the command of Lord Astley was defeated at Stow-on-the-Wolds on 21 March whilst Lord Fairfax was advancing towards the King's headquarters at Oxford to begin the final siege. Charles' military options were now at an end, but there was a political game he might try to play. On the morning of 5 May, the King arrived at Southwell, near Newark, disguised as a clergyman and accompanied by two companions. He

27 British Library, *Moderate Intelligencer*, 8–15 January 1646. See also Wood, *Nottinghamshire Civil War*, Chapter X, pp. 107–21.

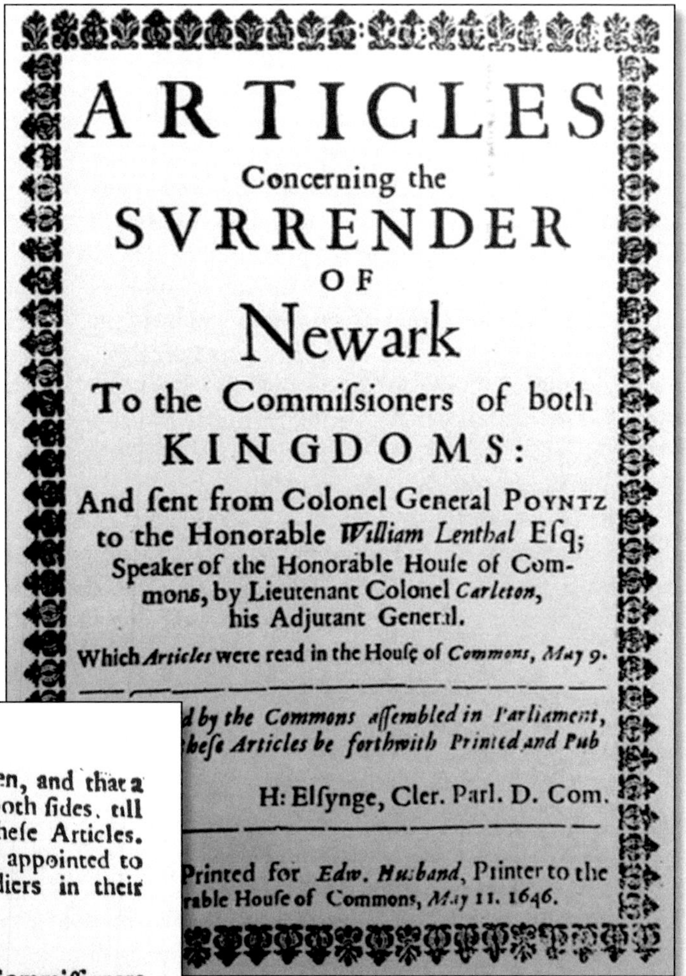

ARTICLES
Concerning the
SVRRENDER
OF
Newark
To the Commiſsioners of both
KINGDOMS:
And ſent from Colonel General POYNTZ
to the Honorable *William Lenthal* Eſq;
Speaker of the Honorable Houſe of Commons, by Lieutenant Colonel *Carleton*,
his Adjutant General.
Which *Articles* were read in the Houſe of *Commons*, *May* 9.

…d by the Commons aſſembled in Parliament,
…heſe Articles be forthwith Printed and Pub…

H: Elſynge, Cler. Parl. D. Com.

Printed for *Edw. Husband*, Printer to the
…rable Houſe of Commons, *May* 11. 1646.

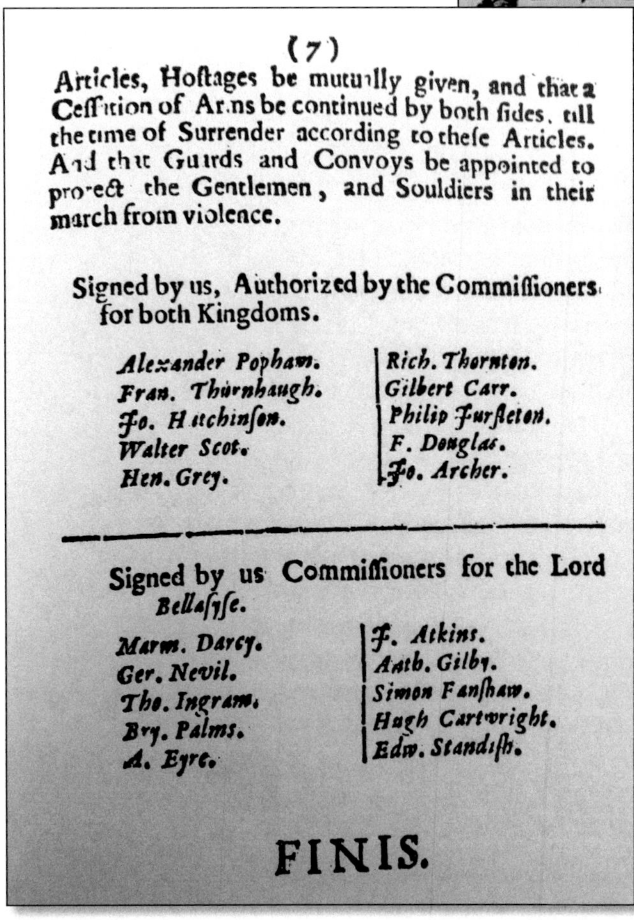

(7)

Articles, Hoſtages be mutually given, and that a Ceſſation of Arms be continued by both ſides, till the time of Surrender according to theſe Articles. And that Guards and Convoys be appointed to protect the Gentlemen, and Souldiers in their march from violence.

Signed by us, Authorized by the Commiſſioners for both Kingdoms.

Alexander Popham.	*Rich. Thornton.*
Fran. Thornhaugh.	*Gilbert Carr.*
Jo. Hutchinſon.	*Philip Jurfleton.*
Walter Scot.	*F. Douglas.*
Hen. Grey.	*Jo. Archer.*

Signed by us Commiſſioners for the Lord *Bellaſyſe.*

Marm. Darcy.	*J. Atkins.*
Ger. Nevil.	*Anth. Gilby.*
Tho. Ingram.	*Simon Fanſhaw.*
Bry. Palms.	*Hugh Cartwright.*
A. Eyre.	*Edw. Standiſh.*

FINIS.

Contemporary pamphlet recording the Articles of Surrender for Newark and the signatories to it. Colonels Francis Thornhagh and John Hutchinson are the second and third individuals to sign on behalf of Parliament. (Author's collection)

believed that by surrendering to the Scots he might be able to form a wedge between them and Parliament. His appearance before Newark proved to be an uncomfortable shock to the Scots and a complete surprise to Poyntz, Thornhagh and the other senior officers in the Parliamentarian forces before the town. This gamble proved to be disastrous both for the King and for the Royalist garrison at Newark for he was persuaded to issue an order to the Governor of the town to surrender at once to the besieging forces. In no position to deny their King, they signed surrender terms the next day on 6 May. The prominence of Thornhagh and Hutchinson, amongst the forces before Newark was such that they both, as commissioners for Parliament, signed the terms of surrender for the garrison.

The King was now a prisoner of the Scots, though there survives no evidence as to what Thornhagh made of this. A few Royalist garrisons continued to hold out for what was now a lost cause; Oxford surrendered on 13 July and the last garrison to surrender was that at Harlech Castle in Wales, which capitulated on 15 March 1647.

Colonel Francis Thornhagh, though twice wounded in battle, had survived the First Civil War. He now faced the task, along with others, of creating a lasting peace over a period of great unease across the country.

5

Member of Parliament and Supporter of the Army's Cause, 1646–1648

On 1 January 1646, Parliament issued an order 'That a Warrant shall issue forth, under Mr. Speaker's Hand, directed to the Clerk of the Crown in Chancery, to issue forth a Writ, for the new Election of Two Burgesses for the Town of Retford, in the places of the Lord Mansfield and Sir Gervase Clifton'.[1]

The fact that the area was severely affected by the presence of two armies undertaking the siege of Royalist Newark meant that the election could not be held until the end of February or beginning of March. On 4 March, the result of the election was published noting that 'Colonel Francis Thornhagh of Fenton, Esq. and Sir William Lister of York [were elected] in place of Sir Gervase Clifton of Clifton and Charles Viscount Mansfield'.[2] Both of the former MP's had been stripped of their status because of their support for the Royalist cause. Charles Cavendish was the eldest son of the Marquis of Newcastle and served as his father's Captain General of Artillery over the years 1642–1644 whilst Sir Gervase Clifton was a Royalist Commissioner of Array and was based at Newark for much of the war.[3] How the election was conducted in the town is difficult to gauge as both Thornhagh, who was a senior army officer besieging Newark and Lister, residing at York, would have found it difficult to have spent much, if any, time at Retford over the election. As voting in the town was restricted to the burgesses, a group of between 50 and 100 men, and at the start of the war the Corporation expressed Parliamentarian sympathies, it probably wasn't too great a surprise that the election yielded these results.[4]

1 HC Journal, IV, 1 January 1646, p. 394.

2 NA, East Retford Parliamentary Election returns, DD/HO/18/2.

3 I am indebted to my colleague Professor Martyn Bennett for drawing my attention to this information.

4 D. Marcombe, *English Small Town Life: Retford, 1520–1642* (Nottingham: University of Nottingham, 1993), pp. 68–91.

Thornhagh wasn't free to attend the Commons until the task at Newark was completed. His first recorded presence at Parliament was on 27 May 1646 when, along with 10 other new MPs, he is recorded as having taken the 'National League and Covenant', presumably prior to taking up his seat in the House. He was to remain at Parliament until 5 October when the Commons Journal recorded that 'Colonel Thornhagh, a Member of this House, shall have Leave to go into the country'.[5] The probable reason for this permission lay in the fact that there were issues relating to the administration and finances of the Nottinghamshire horse, whose services Parliament had retained at the end of the siege of Newark, which required the presence of their commander to resolve. Personal matters may also have played a part in this decision. On 27 September 1646 a third daughter, Frances, was christened at St Peter's Parish Church in Nottingham.[6] The registry entry suggests that Francis may not have been present, but the need to return to his wife and growing young family as soon as possible to support them was also recognised. The fact that Frances died in infancy may imply that the child was frail from birth. St Peter's was a church that had been a centre for puritanism prior to the Civil War and again suggests where Thornhagh's religious sympathies lay.

Another area of responsibility that Thornhagh had to balance alongside his military and parliamentary duties was as a member of the Nottingham county committee. Over the period 4 July 1646 to 29 January 1648, he was one of the members appointed to examine petitions for pensions from wounded soldiers and war widows who had been part of the Nottinghamshire Parliamentarian forces. As commander of the Nottinghamshire horse, it was probably an important task required of him to fulfil. Surviving petitions show that he was present at six cases in 1646, 16 towards the latter part of 1647 and just one in January 1648. These hearings were usually held at Nottingham and so the Colonel would have been absent from Parliament to attend them. The petition of William Spry (29 September 1646) is particularly interesting as it appears that the petitioner approached one of the county's members at Westminster (which one isn't clear) and Francis Pierrepont, Francis Thornhagh, Gervase Pigott and Gilbert Millington (all Nottinghamshire MPs) signed a letter to the county commission asking them to re-examine the case.[7]

This balancing act of politics and army duties was to characterise Thornhagh's public life over the next two years, and in so doing shape or re-affirm both his allegiances and religious sympathies in a way that possibly had not been demanded of him before. The personal financial issues that had also beset Thornhagh in his support of the Parliament again came to prominence over this period, but as we shall see, they remained unresolved over these years.

5 HC Journal, IV, 27 May 1646, p. 556., 5 October 1646, p. 684.

6 NA, St Peters Parish Register, Nottingham, PR 3630, 27 September 1646.

7 <http://www.civilwarpetitions.ac.uk>, accessed 15 May 2019. The petitioners were: John Ashon (4 July 1646); Christopher Barsey, Richard Taylor (12 August 1646) Elizabeth Farnsworth (27 August 1646); Anne Nethercoates (28 August 1646) William Spry (29 September 1646); John Ashon (15 May 1647); Margaret Clarke (27 August 1647); Katherine Hayward, Mrs Rowland (26 October 1647); Elizabeth Farmer, Anne Hill, Elizabeth Newham, Winifred Hill (6 November 1647); Bridget Meanall, Margaret Newton (27 November 1647); Mary Alcocke, Margaret Whittington, Margaret Robinson, widow Norwood, Jane Barton, Elizabeth Dixon (6 December 1647); James Hoe (29 January 1648).

It is each of these areas, military, political and financial that this chapter will now turn to.

Military and Financial Issues, 1646–1647

In his book *Nottinghamshire in the Civil War*, Professor Wood wrote, 'It took only a few days to transform Newark from a beleaguered fortress to an open town once more'.[8]

This was, in fact, a total misreading of the situation for at its surrender, plague was raging within Newark and there was a very real concern that this might spread across the county, shattering an already severely damaged economy. The Scottish army had withdrawn from the siege towards Newcastle, taking the King with them, on 7 May and Poyntz and leaders of the other county forces involved in the final siege withdrew their forces as soon as was possible so as to avoid them also becoming infected. It was left to the Nottinghamshire forces of Hutchinson and Thornhagh to patrol the town and attempt to restrict travel either from or across the area so as to contain the plague. The travel restrictions appear to have been strictly enforced, as far as was possible, and a number of local Royalists still within the town had to plead for extensions and special considerations to the committee for compounding because they were unable to come to pay their fines and lift the sequestrations on their estates 'because of the plague'. In spite of all these efforts, the plague continued to spread out from Newark and the Goose Fair at Nottingham had to be cancelled in October 1646.[9] As late as 25 December 1646, the minutes of the Nottingham Corporation recorded 'Newark – It is thought fitt that the corne comeing from Newark bee not stopped, but household goods to bee stopt that come from thence'.[10]

As Colonel Thornhagh, a newly elected MP was required to attend Parliament to be sworn in as soon as the siege was lifted, it appears that the initial responsibility for enforcing the quarantine regulations fell upon his Major and Colonel Hutchinson. Over the months May to October, the plague crept ever closer towards Nottingham and Thornhagh's regiment of horse would have been increasingly used to monitor the highways and byways leading towards Nottingham. As Lucy Hutchinson noted though 'Yet it pleased God, that not he [Colonel Hutchinson] nor any of the fresh men caught the infection, which was so raging there that it almost desolated the place'.[11]

After 5 October 1646, Thornhagh returned to Nottingham from London. This was probably required so as to help relieve Colonel Hutchinson of some of the heavy duties of policing the quarantine. Alongside this Thornhagh

8 Wood, *Nottinghamshire Civil War*, p. 138.

9 S. B. Jennings, 'A Miserable, Stinking, Infected Town': Pestilence, Plague and Death in a Civil War Garrison, Newark, 1640–1649', *Midland History*, XXVIII (2003), pp. 51–70.; S. B. Jennings, 'Nottinghamshire 1646: Plague, Disruption of Trade and Commerce and the Cancelling of Goose Fair in the County Town of Nottingham', *Midland History*, 43.2 (2018), pp. 174–89.

10 W. Stevenson & J. H. Brown, *Records of the Borough of Nottingham* (London: Quaritch, 1900), V, p. 245.

11 Keeble, *Lucy Hutchinson*, p. 206.

could also begin to address a number of issues relating to the financing and provisioning of his regiment, which were causing considerable hardship for his men at the time. Finally he had a number of personal matters to attend to including his war-damaged lands and estate that lay only 24 miles to the north of Newark.

Probably the most pressing issue for Thornhagh to address was the growing arrears of pay and lack of provisions for his regiment. This was making it increasingly difficult for the continued functioning and discipline of his troops to be maintained. As soon as the Scots had left Nottinghamshire in May, an attempt was quickly made by local Parliamentarians to incorporate back into their circuit of assessment those parishes that formerly had been under the control of the Scots, or lay too close to the Newark garrison to collect money and provisions from during the extended siege. A surviving warrant dated 10 July 1646 issued by Major Charles White to the constables of Gamston cum West Drayton instructing them to pay for Colonel Thornhagh's regiment 'a weekly assessment of £3.10s to Thomas Pond, the appointed collector for Captain Pendock's troop'.[12] The reality was that most of these parishes had already been stripped of cash and provisions over the past six months and had little left to meet such warrants. West Drayton laid only 10 miles west of Colonel Thornhagh's estate at Fenton and it was possibly hoped that his presence and family connections within the region might just aid the collection of these assessments. Thornhagh, from the experience of returning to his own much-depleted estate, may have had sympathies with the local residents but he had hungry and unpaid soldiers to command and he could ill afford to be lax in collecting assessments.

Thornhagh appears to have been around Nottinghamshire until the start of 1647, but the arrears of pay due to his soldiers and the straightened financial situation across the shire meant that he was unable to do anything more than instigate a temporary reprieve for his troops. In March 1647, the fortifications at Nottingham Castle were dismantled and Colonel Hutchinson's regiment of foot, except for two companies retained at the castle, was disbanded. Hutchinson felt that such a small command did not require the services of a colonel and so resigned as governor but one of his final acts was:

> With the assistance of his fellow Parliament men he procured an order from the Parliament for £5000, that had been levied for the Scotch army, but they departed with too much haste to receive it, to be distributed among the officers and soldiers of his regiment that were disbanded, in part of their arrears; and that it might go farther among them, he himself had none of it[13]

The fact that arrangements were in place to deliver the money to Nottinghamshire, probably made it easier for it to be redirected for such use. This possibly brought a little relief to the shire and meant that in future any assessments that could be collected might go directly to Thornhagh's

12 NUMD, Account Papers relating to the estates of the Dukes of Newcastle, Warrant of Major Charles White, Ne A 98.

13 Keeble, *Lucy Hutchinson,* p. 215.

regiment. On 28 June 1647, the Borough minutes of Nottingham recorded 'Soldiers mony – Colonell Thornhagh and Colonell George Hutchinson sendinge theire letter hither to raise mony for ye soldiers, some Alderman beinge absent, and many of the company, the Maior, Alderman and council present desire tyme to consider of it'.[14]

Even after some reductions, delaying tactics and non-payments continued to plight the attempt to resolve soldier's grievances and needs. By July 1647, Thornhagh's regiment were petitioning Lord Fairfax about their financial plight:

> Your humble petitioners, who have from the beginning of our engagements, which bears dates almost with the beginning of theses wars, served the Parliament almost these five years, and have not received for our service past 6s. per week in mony nor free quarter, one week or another, and that there is at this time due unto the regiment £40,000 and upwards, that we have not received above one months pay; and having for our present accommodation and maintenance no other subsistence, than what a small harassed county of charity (which is malignant) will afford in meat and drink … Our humble request to your Excellency is, that you will recommend our future addresses unto the consideration of the honourable Houses of Parliament, whereby we may obtain the wages of our blood, our arrears, and such present maintenance, at first when we engaged under their service were promised.[15]

The petition was printed with the signatures of Thornhagh's Major, Thomas Saunders, and four of his Captains; John Wright, Philip Pendock, George Palmer, Richard Creed all printed. In the Clarke papers at the Bodleian Library, Oxford there survives a manuscript copy of the petition where the names of many of the soldiers who signed it also recorded.[16]

Thornhagh's battle-hardened regiment of horse had been retained by Parliament for possible future service, but its provisioning received no additional financial help from them. The situation continued to deteriorate for the troopers, in spite of the lengthy petition, and in December 1647 the regiment again wrote to Lord Fairfax claiming that it had only received 14 days' pay in six months and that it would be forced to continue to live at free quarter unless prompt steps were taken to ensure regular payment. They continued in their petition that they received no money whatsoever in Derby and Nottinghamshire because they were already living by free quarter and their inhabitants 'conceive themselves discharged by the ordinance, paying these proportions of the Sixty Thousand Pounds per month'.[17]

Aware of these unfolding financial circumstances of his troops back in Nottinghamshire, Thornhagh increasingly agitated for the right and needs of the army in Parliament and his political activities are explored below. Yet the

14 Stevenson & Brown, *Records of the Borough of Nottingham*, V. P. 252.

15 Sir C. Firth and G. Davies, *The Regimental History of Cromwell's Army*, 2 vols (Oxford: Clarendon Press, 1940), 1, pp. 279–80.

16 Firth & Davies, *Regimental History of Cromwell's regiments*, 1, p. 280. Bodleian Library, Oxford, Clarke MSS.

17 J. Rushworth, *Historical Collections*, 7 vols (London: D.Browne, 1742), VII, p. 930. See also Wood, *Nottinghamshire Civil War*, pp. 144–5.

Colonel was not without financial difficulties of his own. By October 1647, he was petitioning the House for the sum of £1,030, this being the amount that he had expended on behalf of the cause during 1643 in raising and equipping a regiment of horse. This was a significant sum of money for his impoverished estate to have to carry. Using a simple 'purchasing power calculator' this would have been equivalent to a sum of £171,600 in 2018. This figure is arrived at by multiplying the initial figure by the estimated percentage increase in the RPI (retail price index) from 1646–2018. This issue would not be resolved during the Colonel's life time and it was left to his widow and influential friends after 1649 to get some, if not all, of this money back (see chapter 7). Like his men, Thornhagh was not receiving his pay also and by August 1649, the treasurers at war at Westminster calculated that he was owed £358.8s.[18] It is possible that Thornhagh's own financial difficulties over arrears made his command over his troops more acceptable, but no less uncomfortable for them. His political siding with the army in Parliament would most certainly have endeared him to them.

Politics and Religion, 1646–1647

Due to military and county committee duties, Colonel Thornhagh spent only weeks at Parliament in the year he was elected as an MP (1646). The following year was to prove as different again with Thornhagh finding himself caught up not only with many parliamentary committees but also with the growing rift between Political Presbyterian and Political Independent factions within the House over the treatment of the army. In fact, one modern historian has claimed 'The English Revolution began in the summer of 1647. It was a struggle to delimit power and authority which nether the constitutional reforms of 1641, nor the Civil War that followed had been able to resolve'.[19]

Over the 12 months of 1647, the Colonel was to find his loyalties to army and Parliament and his religious sympathies tested and defined by the unfolding events.

By the start of 1647, a growing number of issues caused considerable concern for the conservative Political Presbyterian majority within the Commons. These included the growing religious radicalism within the army, the escalating burden of taxation required to sustain the army and finally the ongoing rebellion in Ireland that still needed to be suppressed. Both within Parliament and across the shires there was a desire to return the country back to its pre-war social structures via a negotiated treaty with the King. For the army though other matters weighed heavily, amongst which lay the issues of unpaid arrears, guarantees of indemnity for actions taken in Parliament's name over the course of the Civil War, religious freedoms and the threat of compulsory conscription to serve in Ireland. For the ordinary soldiers there could be no questioning of disbanding regiments until these matters were

18 HC Journal, VI, 17 August 1649, p. 280.

19 M. A. Kishlanksy, 'The Army and the Levellers: The Road to Putney', *The Historical Journal*, Vol. 22, No. 4 (December, 1979), p. 795.

Facsimile of Francis Thornhagh's signature, which from the end of 1646 began to appear on many documents both at Parliament and back in Nottinghamshire. (Author's collection)

addressed.[20] This then was the backcloth to events for the first seven months of 1647, which were to culminate in decisive action taken by the army in August.

Thornhagh returned to Westminster in early January 1647 after a period of weeks in Nottinghamshire and on 21 January he was appointed by the House to sit on the committee that was to 'consider of Instructions to be given to the Judges, to be made use of them at the Assizes, in the Circuits, this next visitation'.[21] With the fighting now ended across the country, the law courts could once again begin to operate and cases heard around the regions. At such Assizes, soldiers could possibly also find themselves presented by individuals for actions taken over the war, reinforcing for them the need for an indemnity bill passed by the Parliament. A few weeks later, on 4 February, Thornhagh found himself appointed by the House to a committee to prepare a declaration 'to prevent the Resort and Tumultuous Addresses of all Disbanded Soldiers to the Parliament'.[22] Large numbers of disbanded soldiers, owed considerable arrears of pay for their service, gathered outside Parliament to petition for their owed back pay. The presence of so many and the nature of their petitioning were proving to be both tumultuous and intimidating to MPs as they went about their business. Thornhagh would have not approved of this threat to social order but neither would have he been unsympathetic to the soldier's financial plight, having witnessed the deprivations such debts caused for men in his own regiment. His reservations would have been confirmed the next month, when the Political Presbyterians in Parliament used this legislation as an excuse not to receive the petition from the New Model army requesting the authorities to honour their faithful service by addressing their escalating arrears of pay.[23]

The final significant committee appointment, Thornhagh served on, prior to the major rift between the army and Parliament was that established on 27 February to facilitate and execute the parliamentary ordinance 'for the sale of the Bishop's Lands'.[24] This was to be a considerable undertaking as questions about the identification of lands, legality of sales and the rights of sitting tenants all had to legislated for. The Colonel is also mentioned on two other occasions in the Commons Journal prior to the intervention of the army, as a vote teller on 1 March and to a committee to consider the case of Sir Richard Pryce on

20 For a detailed discussion of these issues see Kishlanksy, 'The Army and the Levellers' pp. 795–824.

21 HC Journal, V, 21 January 1649, p. 60.

22 HC Journal, V, 4 February 1649, p. 75.

23 Kishlanksy, 'The Army and the Levellers' pp. 798–9.

24 HC Journal, V, 27 February 1649, p. 99.

8 July. The latter case is not detailed in the journal minutes but may have been related to the issue of MPs receiving irregular payments.[25]

The growing conflict between the army and the Commons escalated after the latter rejected the army petition in April 1647 and then rather rashly decided to proceed with their plans to disband the army, deprive some higher ranked officers of their command, send some of the remaining regiments to Ireland and all without any commitment to meeting their arrears of pay. On 25 May, Parliament ordered the disbanding to go ahead and on 4 June 1647, the army responded by holding a rendezvous at Newmarket and the next day soldiers and officers bound themselves by a *Solemne Engagement* to remain together until their demands were met. The army's trust in Parliament to address their grievances was shattered and politicians of an Independent persuasion who had sympathies with the army began to fear a return to arbitrary government and religious persecution under the political Presbyterian majority. Amongst this former group was Francis Thornhagh, whose own regiment of horse had marched south to Buckingham to join up with Sir Thomas Fairfax.[26]

Although Thornhagh had been required to swear the *National League and Covenant* prior to taking up his seat in Parliament, there remains no evidence to suggest that his own religious preference was for a strict form of Presbyterianism. His closest friend, John Hutchinson, was certainly Independent in his religious outlook and within his own regiment there was also a strong Independent religious spirit that Thornhagh did little to suppress. The newspaper *Mercurius Elencticus* published an account for November 1647, by which time the Nottinghamshire horse had returned to their own county, gives an insight into the religious sympathies of some of Thornhagh's troops:

> From Newark tis certified lately that a party of Colonel Thornhagh's men endeavoured lately to hinder the reading of the Common Prayer Book; but the resolute and religious dames of the town fell upon them, beat them forth of the church, and afterwards performed their devotions in despite of the cowards. A fair testimony to the perseverance of that loyal town in their obedience and loyalty.[27]

It might be argued that the soldiers were doing nothing more than enforcing an ordinance forbidding the use of the prayer book, but given the entrenched Royalist sympathies of that town and the zeal with which the soldiers tried to disrupt proceedings, it does suggests that Thornhagh's troops were doing more than just following orders.

On 25 July 1647, demonstrators, including a number of London's apprentices, assembled around Westminster clamouring for peace to be made with the King and the disbandment of the army. Although tensions had been running high between certain sections of Parliament and the army, in recent weeks there had been signs that the former had begun trying to pacify the angst

25 HC Journal, V, 1 March 1649, 102; 8 July 1647, p. 238.

26 Wood, *Nottinghamshire Civil War*, p. 144.

27 *Mercurius Elencticus*, 12–19 November 1647, British Library E.416[13], p.21. See also Firth, *Memoirs of Colonel Hutchinson*, p. 242. footnote 1.

of the army. Supported by the crowds, the leaders of the Political Presbyterian faction in the House were able to persuade the Parliament to return control of the London militia back to Presbyterian members and also to pass a resolution to ask the King to return to London. All of these actions sought to diminish the threat of the army, but in fact they brought the divisions to a head, forcing politicians to finally take sides. On 27 July 57 Political Independent MPs, eight Peers and the Speakers from both from the Commons and the Lords, after issuing a declaration, fled from Westminster and sought the protection of Fairfax and the army. Amongst this group were the Nottinghamshire MPs Francis Pierrepont, John Hutchinson and Francis Thornhagh.

The lengthy declaration issued by these Independent members on 4 August was recorded in the Journal of the House of Lords on their return to their seats on 13 August 1647. It began with a justification for taking their action 'We the members of both Houses of Parliament, who do absent ourselves from the service of the Parliament by reason of the Force and Violence offered thereunto by a tumultuous Mulitude.'

They then go one to explain why the Declaration issued by the army 'Sheweing the Grounds of their present Advancement towards the City of London' persuaded them to side with the army cause. What followed was a mixture of both pragmatism and flattery towards the army:

> And generally throughout our Sense so fully agreed with what is expressed in that Declaration of the Army, that we cannot but receive it with much Approbation; and also with great Thankfulness to God in the first place, and next under Him to this ever-faithful Army, for that tender Sense expressed therein of our Honour and Security ... Whereupon we cannot but mutually engage ourselves, as hereby we do, to live and die with Sir Thomas Fairfax and this Army, in the Vindication of the Honour and Freedom of the Parliament.

To this statement of religious belief in the political cause of the army, all the absent members added their signatures, including Thornhagh, Hutchinson and Pierrepont.[28]

The army entered London on 6 August and the city's militia offered no resistance. Most of the 11 leaders of the Presbyterian faction identified by the army had already fled from the capital and those that hadn't were removed from Parliament by the army. The army's intervention allowed the 58 members who had fled to Fairfax for protection to return to the Commons to take up their seats again. The army allowed the remainder of MPs in Parliament to continue with their business whilst it retired to its new headquarters at Putney, in the county of Surrey. Here from 28 October through to 11 November a series of debates involving senior army officers, agitators (representatives) appointed by the various regiments and civilian Leveller leaders sought to arrive at a new constitution for Britain. No agreement was reached and the escape of the King from Hampton Court on 11 November brought the debates

28 Journal of the House of Lords, hereafter HL Journal (London: HMSO, 1767–1830), 9, 13 August 1647, pp. 385–6.

to a swift end. Although Francis Thornhagh was a trusted army officer, and his regiment had thrown in their lot with Fairfax, there are no surviving records to show that either was involved directly in the Putney Debates.[29]

Over the summer and autumn of 1647, as the rupture between the army and Parliament came to a head, the contrasting responses of Thornhagh and his former commander Sydenham Poyntz, of the Northern Association, was to take them along very different camps. It also appears that Thornhagh had more of an ear to the prevailing mood of his soldiers. Within the Presbyterian faction in London, Poyntz had been identified as a commander, who with his troops, might act as a counterpoint to the independent spirits in the New Model army. Their hope was to prove ill founded, for unknown to Poyntz his troops had already been in contact with the soldiers of Fairfax's army and had appointed agitators to represent them. On 8 July 1647, Poyntz was seized by his own men and sent as a prisoner to Fairfax's headquarters charged with 'endeavouring to embroil the kingdom on a new war'. Fairfax eventually released him but he was stripped of his command and Colonel Lambert was appointed to take his place.[30] The consequence of this series of events for Thornhagh and the Nottinghamshire horse was to bring them into a close relationship with Oliver Cromwell. From the end of 1647 until his death in August 1648, Thornhagh and his regiment served under the command of Cromwell rather than the newly appointed General John Lambert and the Northern army.

Whilst Francis Thornhagh appears to have remained detached, but not uninformed, from the debates within the army at Putney, as a trusted MP he again quickly found himself appointed to a number of significant parliamentary committees over the autumn of 1647. On 1 October, he was co-opted on to an already sitting committee appointed to consider 'the Payment of the Twenty-eight thousand Pounds to divers reduced and reformed officers'. This enlarged committee was also charged with the additional responsibilities of identifying 'frauds and abuses' amongst claimants, methods by which this money could be raised and finally consideration of whom should be awarded such payments. Given that arrears of pay to the army had been a catalyst for the friction between the army and Presbyterians in Parliament, the work of this committee took on renewed importance. The addition of a further thirteen army officers to this committee probably ensured that it did make some progress on this issue, especially with regard to the New Model army. Thornhagh's experience of hearing petitions for pensions and grants from widows and soldiers in Nottinghamshire would have made him a useful addition to this committee. It is probably not without coincidence that within days of being appointed to this body, Thornhagh's own claim for outstanding expenses owed in forming his regiment of horse was presented to Parliament.[31]

Though the 11 MPs identified as leaders of the Presbyterian faction had been removed from Parliament by the army, the Commons still sought to conduct

29 Further details can be found in Kishlanksy, 'The Army and the Levellers', pp. 795–824.

30 C. H. Firth, 'Sydenham Poyntz' in *Dictionary of National Biography* (London: Smith, Elder and Co, 1885–1900), Vol. 46.

31 HC Journal, V, 1 October 1647, p. 322.

its own negotiations with the King alongside those of the army grandees. On 6 October, Thornhagh was appointed to the committee established 'to consider and prepare a Proposition, according to the Debate now had in the House, to be sent to the King for his consent, concerning the settlement of the Presbyterian Government [of the church] and concerning the Exemption of such tender Consciences as cannot conform to that Government'.[32] Again Thornhagh's political and religious sympathies, which tended towards independency, would have made him a useful spokesperson for those of 'tender consciences'. These negotiations were quickly brought to a halt by the escape of the King from his army gaolers at Hampton Court on 11 November.

The Journey Towards a Second Civil War

Trust between the four negotiating parties (Parliament, army, the Scots and the King) had never been well established and even within each of these parties there were further divisions. The Scots were particularly concerned about the King being held by the army and the rise of Independent influence within the English Parliament. They feared these factors might lead to the breaking of the agreement to establish a Presbyterian form of church government as agreed in the Solemn League and Covenant of 1643. Likewise in the minds of the army and Independent members of Parliament there was a growing concern that the King and Scots might form an alliance against them. Attitudes within the army began to change and amongst the King's warders at Hampton Court behaviour towards Charles became less respectful and more restrictive. On 11 November his army guardian, Edward Whalley, showed the King some correspondence he had received from Oliver Cromwell warning of 'some murderous design, or fear of it, against his Majesty'.[33] The consequence was that Charles brought forward plans to escape from his captors to that same evening. The escape plan, perhaps because it was brought forward, was an abysmal failure and within two days he found himself again a prisoner, this time at Carisbrooke Castle on the Isle of Wight. Here he did enjoy some relaxation of his confinement and was able to still meet up with representatives of the different parties. On 25 December 1647, the King signed an *Engagement* with the Scots in which he promised to support the establishment of a Presbyterian Church structure in England for three years in return for military support from the Scots against the army and Independents. The fact the Charles himself refused to take the covenant or force others to do so, split the Scottish Parliament and Kirk, with a number fearing he would not honour this agreement once returned to power.

Thornhagh's contrasting roles within Parliament and the army would have kept him well informed of the deteriorating situation. It must have been with a mixture of dismay and disappointment that he viewed the forthcoming year of 1648.

32 HC Journal, V, 6 October 1647, p. 327.

33 British Library, Thomason Tract, TTS 416/23), *Whalley's Letter to the Speaker of the Commons.*

6

Francis Thornhagh and the Second Civil War, 1648

The events of January 1648 were to have a significant impact upon the future fortunes of both Francis Thornhagh and his wider family. A son and heir to Francis, by the name of John, was baptised at St Mary's parish church, Nottingham on the 28th of the month. At the beginning of the month on 3 January, the Commons had voted by 141 to 91 to pass the *Vote of No Address* and sever all future negotiations with the King. After news of the King's engagement with the Scots became known, coupled with his rejection of Parliament's bills, the Commons felt they had little choice but to break off all negotiations. Not only was trust in Charles at an all-time low, there was also growing animosity towards the Scots. Also on 3 January, Parliament dissolved the Committee for Both Kingdoms, bringing to an end the cooperation in affairs between England and Scotland. With the Lord's sanctioning of the *Vote of No Address* on 17 January and the Scottish Commissioners leaving London on 24 January, the road to future conflict lay open. The fact that Thornhagh continued to serve as commander of his regiment and as an MP ensured that he would find himself significantly caught up with events as they subsequently unfolded.

Colonel Francis Thornhagh: From Peace to the Siege of Pembroke Castle

In spite of the gathering war clouds, Parliament sought to continue with its everyday business. Concerns about the ongoing rebellion in Ireland, led the Commons at the start of February to pass legislation to raise from across the country the additional sum of £20,000 per month by assessment to fund further military assistance to their thinly stretched forces already in Ireland. The county of Nottinghamshire was assessed at £117.19s.9d per month of which the town of Nottingham was to pay £3.18s.2s. The trusted Colonel

Thornhagh was appointed to oversee the raising of the county's levy.[1] How successful he was in setting up and initiating this assessment before military duties called him away to serve under Cromwell remains unclear.

Alongside the machinations of the King, Scots and political Presbyterians in Parliament, there also existed a growing popular resentment against the high levels of taxation needed to sustain the army, the growing interference of puritan views upon popular culture and, also the perceived 'tyranny' of county committees. Christmas 1647 saw riots in a number of cities and towns as county authorities tried to compel shop and markets to remain open, whilst seasonal church services were suppressed. The disbandment of 20,000 soldiers by Parliament in February 1648 did little to defuse the growing dissatisfaction about taxation or stem a popular desire for the return of the King and the former ways of governance. All of this was to feed into a series of uncoordinated revolts across southern England and Wales that preceded the invasion of a Scottish army and became known as the second Civil War. Being at Nottingham over the months of December and January, Thornhagh would have been alerted to this growing anger as he witnessed popular discontent with the borough corporation attempts to implement new parliamentary legislation. Disturbances were considerably less than those witnessed at towns such as Canterbury, Ipswich and London, but nevertheless they were alarming.[2]

Although popular discontent was rising, possibly stirred up by Royalist sympathisers, it was the attempt to disband Parliamentarian soldiers in Wales that sparked the conflict. Troops under the command of Major General Laugharne and Colonel Poyer were extremely unhappy with the terms offered to them for disbanding. On 22 February 1648, when Adjutant General Fleming arrived to replace Poyer as governor of Pembroke, the latter, supported by his men, refused to hand over the castle. In response, Parliament passed an ordinance on 3 March declaring both Poyer and his troops to be traitors unless they surrendered immediately to Fleming.[3] The rebellion at Pembroke Castle soon attracted the support of other disaffected Parliamentarian soldiers and officers, including Rowland Laugharne and Colonel Rice Powell. This act of defiance took a more ominous direction when on 23 March Poyer and his associates declared for the King and the restoration of the *Prayer Book* across South Wales.[4] Within a month of Poyer's declaration, on 18 April, the Scottish Parliament resolved to raise an army against their English counterpart. This declaration further stimulated a series of uncoordinated Royalist uprisings across England over the months of May and June.

It lies beyond the scope of this biography to provide a full history of the Second Civil War. Instead, it will focus on those events that involve

---

1 Firth and Rait, *Acts and Ordinances, I*, 16 February 1648, pp. 1072–1105.

2 I. Gentles, *The English Revolution and the Wars in the Three Kingdoms, 1638–1652* (London; Pearson Education, 2007), pp. 328–33.

3 HL Journal, 10, 3 March 1648, p. 89.

4 P. Gaunt, *A Nation Under Siege: The Civil War in Wales, 1642–48* (London: Cadw, 1991), pp. 66–71.

Colonel Thornhagh and the Nottinghamshire horse, which served throughout the war under the command of Lieutenant General Oliver Cromwell. By the early spring of 1648, several troops of the Nottinghamshire horse were already present on the Welsh and Shropshire border to keep an eye on the area with a further troop quartered at Coventry. In a letter dated 3 May, it was reported that 'in Herefordshire Major Saunders [Thornhagh's second in command] hath quelled the malignants there and taken Col. Sherington Talbot prisoner'. Colonel Thomas Horton reported on 6 May that 'Capt. Creed with three troops of Col. Thornhaugh's regiment doth very good service … being now quartered about Glasbury bridge, which is a good pass near the conjunction of the counties of Hereford, Radnor and Brecon'.

By 17 June, Cromwell was issuing orders from the siege at Pembroke to Major Saunders to move from Brecknockshire into Glamorganshire to seize Sir Trevor Williams of Llangibby and Mr Morgan, High Sheriff of Monmouth, both of whom were described as 'dangerous plotters'.[5]

Oliver Cromwell. From May 1648 through to his death on 18 August, Colonel Francis Thornhagh and his regiment were to serve under Cromwell's command. (Image from John Vicars, *England's Worthies*, London: John Russell Smith, 1845)

On 30 April 1648, Cromwell was ordered to take a detachment of the New Model army, consisting of two regiments of horse and three of foot, to join Colonel Horton in putting down the rebellion in south Wales. He left London on 3 May and reached Gloucester on 8 May. It was probably here that Colonel Thornhagh and the remaining troops of his regiment, which had been ordered to serve under Cromwell on this campaign, joined him.[6] The absence of the Nottinghamshire horse left the shire vulnerable to attempts by Lord Byron and a small force of Royalists to take Nottingham castle, which then was only guarded by a greatly reduced Parliamentarian garrison. Further Royalist activities within Nottinghamshire were thwarted with the help of the Lincolnshire forces under Colonel Rossiter.[7]

From Gloucester, Thornhagh marched with Cromwell to occupy Chepstow on 11 May. Leaving Colonel Ewer and his regiment to besiege the castle, the rest of army moved on to Cardiff, arriving there on 15 May and Swansea by 19 May. Cromwell finally arrived at Pembroke Castle to begin his siege on 24 May. As they were progressing through south Wales, Parliament's thoughts, concerns and plans were increasingly turned towards the border regions and Scotland. On 29 April, Marmaduke Langdale with a force of Royalists occupied Berwick in the name of the King, preparing for the arrival of a Scottish army. It wasn't until 8 July though, that the Duke of Hamilton

5 Firth and Davies, *Regimental History of Cromwell's Army,* 1, pp. 280–1.

6 P. Gaunt, *Oliver Cromwell* (Oxford: Blackwells, 1996), pp. 93–94. Also Martyn Bennett, *Cromwell at War: The Lord General and his Military Revolution* (London: I.B. Tauris, 2017), pp. 147–52.

7 Keeble, *Lucy Hutchinson,* pp. 219–21. See also *Moderate Intelligencer*, May 11–18, 1648.

Pembroke Castle, where Colonel Thornhagh and at least two troops of the Nottinghamshire horse were involved in the siege under the command of General Cromwell. (Photo: Hugh-John Wilson, with permission)

felt ready to march his army over the border from Scotland in support of the King's cause. Parliament had set in place provisions to prepare for this invasion, weeks before it actually happened. On 19 May, just as Cromwell arrived at Swansea, Lord Fairfax informed the Commons about the disposal of forces to suppress the various insurrections. Amongst these details, he notes:

> I hear that Lieutenant General Cromwell out of his own regiment and Colonel Thornhagh's, hath sent Five Troops of Horse, together with some Dragoons to the confines of Shropshire, Cheshire and North Wales, to whom I shall now send orders to join with Colonel Harrison against the enemy in Lancashire.[8]

On this occasion, Thornhagh probably remained with the remainder of his regiment moving on towards Pembroke Castle.

The siege of Pembroke (24 May–11 July 1648) proved to be a much longer affair than Cromwell had anticipated. The castle was well defended and equipped with a secret water supply, which was not discovered and cut off until near the end of the siege. It was also able to resist two attempts to be stormed by Cromwell on 7 and 27 June.[9] Thereafter, Cromwell and his officers decided to try and starve the Pembroke rebels out of the castle rather than risk further casualties with direct assaults. On 1 July heavy siege guns arrived at Milford Haven and by 4 July Cromwell was able to commence a heavy bombardment of the castle. A mixture of starvation and artillary fire finally forced Poyer and Laugharne to surrender Pembroke on 11 July 1648.

In a siege, such as at Pembroke, cavalry were of limited use compared to infantry and sappers. A number would have been retained for foraging and dealing with any attempted breakouts by the besieged enemy and also guarding against the arrival of a relief force. On 5 June 1648, Parliament

8 HL Journal, 10, 19 May 1648, p. 267.
9 Gaunt, *Nation under Siege* pp. 66–71. Bennett, *Cromwell at War*, 148–51.

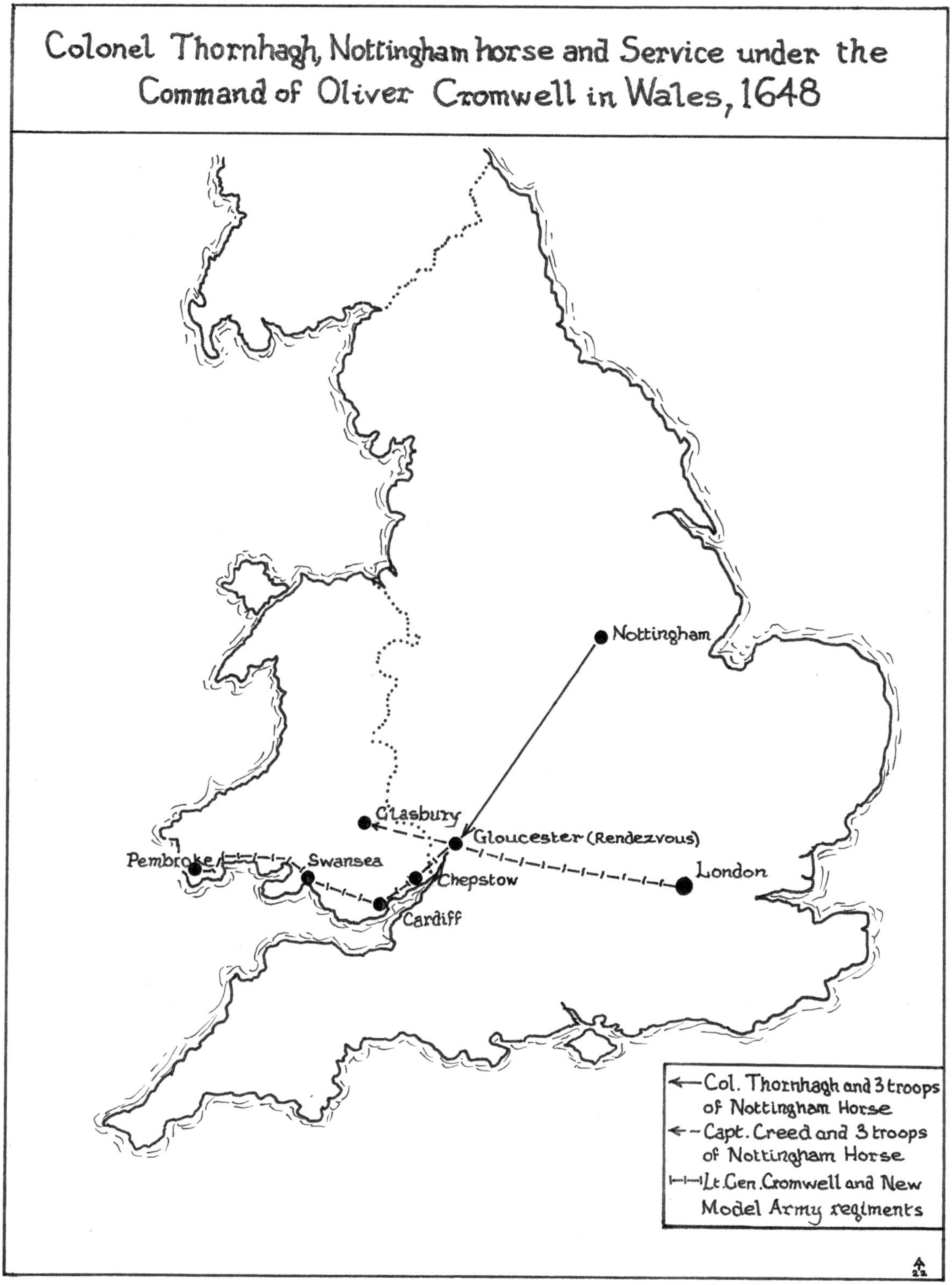
Colonel Thornhagh, Nottingham horse and Service under the Command of Oliver Cromwell in Wales, 1648
Nottingham
Glasbury
Gloucester (Rendezvous)
London
Pembroke
Swansea
Chepstow
Cardiff
Col. Thornhagh and 3 troops of Nottingham Horse
Capt. Creed and 3 troops of Nottingham Horse
Lt. Gen. Cromwell and New Model Army regiments

received a report from Cromwell in which he stated that he had given an order 'to Colonel Ewer to march with his regiment to Coventry and had sent thither also two troops of Thornhagh's Horse'.[10] It is unclear whether Thornhagh remained with the rest of his regiment (possibly two troops) or went with the two troops to Coventry. Given the Colonel's previous record of desiring to be at the centre of action, and the very emotional goodbyes made later at Nottingham (see below), it seems most likely that he remained at Pembroke until the castle surrendered. This might also explain the growing awareness and respect that both Cromwell and Thornhagh developed for one another. It is probable though that at least three troops of Thornhagh's regiment were part of the divisions of cavalry that joined Major General John Lambert's on 27 July to help him track and delay the progress of the Scottish army until Cromwell could join him.

It was not until 16 July that Cromwell felt able to leave Pembroke, taking with him Poyer and Laugharne as prisoners. He returned to England passing through Gloucester and Warwick before arriving at Leicester on 1 August. Here his army received new provisions, including shoes from Northampton and stockings from Coventry, which after the long march would have been essential for his soldiers. Whilst at Leicester he received the news that he had been appointed Commander-in-Chief of all Parliament's forces in the north of England to engage with the Scottish army. He therefore wrote to Lambert, commander of the northern army, instructing him to 'forbear engaging [with the Scots] before he came up'.[11]

Cromwell arrived at Nottingham on 3 August, though it is possible that Thornhagh and the remainder of his regiment had ridden on ahead from Leicester to their own town to help reduce the logistics of quartering across the town of Leicester, which was still probably recovering from its storming in 1645. Cromwell's army was to spend four days at Nottingham before marching the 40 miles to Doncaster, arriving on 8 August. Lucy Hutchinson in her somewhat biased biography of her husband Colonel John Hutchinson, written 20 years later, provides us with some rare insights into events over this time.[12] According to her account, Colonel Hutchinson 'Went to see him [Cromwell], whom he embraced with all expressions of kindness that one friend could make to another, and then retiring with him, with very earnest entreaties pressed him to tell him what thoughts his friends, the Levellers had of him'.[13]

Hutchinson's response was apparently blunt and to the point, which according to Lucy made Cromwell dread him 'and made it his business to keep him out of the army'.

That Cromwell and Hutchinson possibly had an uncomfortable relationship might have proven to be a little awkward for Thornhagh, but it in no way diminished his long-term friendship with Hutchinson. The

10 CSPD, 22, 5 June 1648, p. 101.
11 Bennett, *Cromwell at War*, p. 151.
12 Keeble, *Lucy Hutchinson*, pp. 223–4.
13 Keeble, *Lucy Hutchinson*, p. 223.

Memoirs provide us with a poignant account of their parting in August when Thornhagh left Nottingham with Cromwell to engage the Scottish army.

> … and at his parting with Colonel Hutchinson took such a kind leave of him, with such dear expressions of love and such brotherly embraces and such regrets for any rash jealousies he had been wrought into, that it took a great impression in the Colonel's kind heart, and might have been a presage to him that they should meet no more, when they parted with such extraordinary melting; but that Colonel Hutchinson's cheerful and constant spirit never anticipated any evil with fear.[14]

It is probable that over these few days at Nottingham, Thornhagh made arrangements for his estates and amended his will to provide for his family and the upbringing of his new-born heir should he be killed on this campaign. This may well have added to his emotional state, shown at his parting with his long-term friend John Hutchinson. The instructions were rushed, and the additions to his will caused some problems for his executors and widow later in the year after his death, resulting in depositions having to be taken before the authorities (see chapter 7). Whether or not Thornhagh took a long look back at his home of Nottingham as he rode away to his last battle the records do not say, but knowledge of his character and a little bit of imagination, suggests that he may have done.

The Battle of Preston, 17 August 1648

As Cromwell moved on to Doncaster on 8 August, Thornhagh with what remained of his regiment, possibly two troops of horse went with him. The larger part of his regiment, along with much of Cromwell's horse had been sent up ahead from Wales to support the northern army under General Lambert, arriving on 27 July.[15] Cromwell paused at Doncaster for three days to help coordinate the siege at Pontefract, but whether Thornhagh remained with him or pressed on ahead with his troopers to rendezvous with Lambert's forces again remains unclear.

Cromwell and Lambert's armies came together at Wetherby on 12 August and their combined force probably came to around 12,000 soldiers.[16] The majority of this army consisted of either New Model army veterans or battle-experienced troops such as Thornhagh's regiment of horse. This combined force under the command of Cromwell crossed over the Pennines via the Ribble valley and on 17 August 1648 fell upon the rearguard of the Scottish army outside Preston.

This consisted of mainly English Royalists under the command of Sir Marmaduke Langdale. What has become known as the Battle of Preston, in fact consisted of two major engagements at two different sites. The first

14 Keeble, *Lucy Hutchinson*, p. 223.

15 Firth and Davies, *Regimental History of Cromwell's Army*, 1, p. 281.

16 Gentles, *The English Revolution*, p. 344. The author argues convincingly that the figure was higher than the 8,000 previously claimed by many.

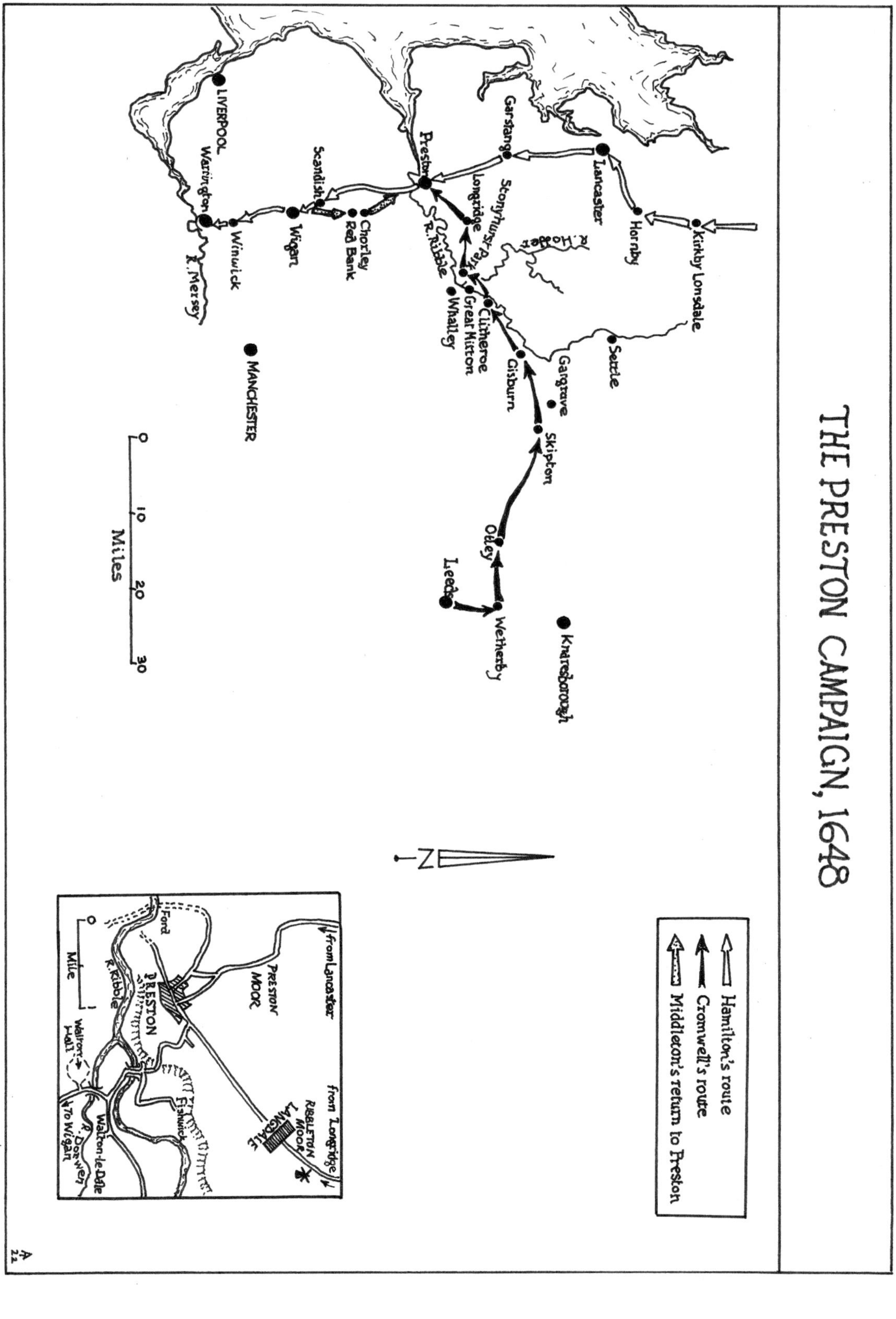
THE PRESTON CAMPAIGN, 1648
Hamilton's route
Cromwell's route
Middleton's return to Preston
Kirkby Lonsdale
Hornby
Lancaster
Garstang
Preston
Stonyhurst Park
Longridge
R. Hodder
R. Ribble
Settle
Gargrave
Clitheroe
Great Mitton
Whalley
Gisburn
Skipton
Otley
Leeds
Wetherby
Knaresborough
Chorley
Red Bank
Standish
Wigan
Winwick
Warrington
R. Mersey
LIVERPOOL
MANCHESTER
0
10
20
30
Miles
N
from Lancaster
PRESTON MOOR
Ford
PRESTON
R. Ribble
from Longridge
RIBBLETON MOOR
LANGDALE
Fishwick
Walton Hall
R. Darwen
Walton-le-Dale
To Wigan
0
1
Mile

occurred on the western edge of Ribbleton Moor and began at around midday and lasted over five hours. The second occurred, after the defeat of Langdale's rearguard, at the bridge over the River Ribble as Cromwell pushed on to confront the bulk of the Scottish foot that had already crossed and lasted for around two hours until darkness fell. The weather that day was atrocious with heavy, driving rain and very muddy conditions underfoot.[17]

The Scottish invasion had finally taken place several weeks too late to aid a series of Royalist uprisings across Wales and England. It had been held up by opposition within the Kirk to the *Engagement*, which Charles had failed to take and led many not to trust him. By the time an army had been raised to crossed over to England, many of its regiments had been filled up to strength with untrained levies, whilst the whole army was short of ammunition, artillery and provisions. As it made its slow progress down towards Lancashire, it had to resort to plunder to feed itself, thus stifling any hope of attracting popular support for the King's cause. The failure of the Scottish commander, the Duke of Hamilton, to engage with the then smaller Parliamentarian force of Lambert and instead take the western route towards Manchester was also to prove critical to his cause. By the time the combined forces of Cromwell and Lambert caught up with the Scottish army outside Preston, Hamilton's army had grown up to around 20,000 horse and foot but was strung out across in a thin line about 20 miles. This was because the Duke had allowed his cavalry to advance ahead of the foot by about 15 miles to Wigan in order to forage for scarce fodder and food.[18]

Cromwell, even with a smaller force, decided to put his army between Hamilton and the road back to Scotland thus ensuring that a military engagement would have to take place. The fact that the Scottish rearguard under Langdale and Hamilton were oblivious to the whereabouts of Cromwell's army until the last moment, helped the Parliamentarians to pull off this strategic manoeuvre. Langdale became aware of Cromwell's proximity on the evening of 16 August and pulled his small rearguard back towards Preston on the morning of 17 August. By mid-morning he had taken up a defensive position outside Preston on the edge of Ribbleton Moor amid the enclosures and hedgerows that were there. He requested help from Hamilton for some of the Scottish foot to strengthen his small force of 3,600 soldiers but either the message didn't get through or Hamilton was persuaded by his other senior officers that this was only the vanguard of Cromwell's force and that he should continue to get his foot over the River Ribble and take up a defensive position there whilst sending a message to Wigan for his cavalry to return.

Hamilton's lack of response to the approach of Cromwell, gave the latter a considerable superiority in numbers over Langdale's forces. Cromwell sent the cavalry of his advance guard in an attempt to rush the Royalist position, as he drew up the rest of his army ready for battle. This initial attack failed because Langdale made effective use of the hedges and enclosures on either

17 A helpful topography of the battlefields is provided by M. Wanklyn, *Decisive Battles of the English Civil War* (Barnsley: Pen and Sword, 2014), pp. 185–9.

18 Gentles, *The English Revolution*, pp. 342–3.

side of the Clitheroe road, which was extremely muddy and narrow. The landscape around Langdale's defensive position made the use of cavalry very difficult in this terrain and in the end the battle came to a bloody contest between the infantry of the New Model army and the forces of Langdale. Not until the latter's force finally broke and fled, did Cromwell's cavalry come into prominence. Thornhagh and Twistleton's regiments of horse formed the right wing of Cromwell's army and although their involvement was limited, they were adjudged to have performed creditably in the tasks allocated to them. Though out-numbered, Langdale's forces put up a resilient defence holding Cromwell up for about five hours but eventually sheer numbers overwhelmed them and they broke and fled. Most of the infantry were killed or captured but the remainder of Langdale's cavalry scattered northward. Cromwell's forces rushed into Preston to secure the town for Parliament.[19]

The bulk of Hamilton's infantry were now assembled in a defensive position on the southern bank of the River Ribble. They were soaked, hungry and probably disheartened at the sight of the destruction of Langdale's forces unfolding before them. Cromwell, sensing the mood, decided to press his advantage and attacked the 600 musketeers left by Hamilton to defend the bridge over the river. After a struggle, culminating in a push of pike, Cromwell's forces took the bridge but further action was halted by the fall of night. By the end of 17 August, Cromwell estimated he had captured around 4,000 of the enemy and killed over a 1,000.[20] With no chance of slipping past Cromwell's forces, which had been strategically placed along the northern bank of the river, Hamilton decided to attempt a night withdrawal of his army southwards to rendezvous with his cavalry under the command of Sir Thomas Middleton. Moving a cold, hungry and exhausted army in the dark, is a difficult manoeuvre to attempt and in the chaos the order to blow up the ammunition wagons, which were too cumbersome and noisy to move silently in the dark, was not passed on allowing them to fall into the hands of Cromwell the next morning.

The Scottish army made its initial withdrawal but once Cromwell was aware he took immediate action. Early on 18 August he gave Thornhagh command of several regiments of horse, including his own Nottinghamshire, to pursue Hamilton's foot and by skirmishes and raids slow down its progress towards Wigan so that the rest of the Parliamentarian army might catch up. The size of Thornhagh's force was probably between 1,400–1,800 troopers. In effect he commanded a brigade, a battlefield appointment that carried no advancement in rank. This was a considerable responsibility allocated to Thornhagh, possibly reflecting Cromwell's growing trust in the young colonel's abilities but probably also because he was the senior colonel at his disposal. Though they initially missed each other in the night, Middleton's Scottish horse caught up with Hamilton and put up a considerable defence as the rearguard to the Scottish foot, as Thornhagh's horse vanguard was to discover.

19 A. Woolrych, *Battles of the English Civil War: Marston Moor, Naseby, Preston* (London: Phoenix Press, 1991), pp. 168–71.

20 Gentles, *The English Revolution*, p. 347.

Looking south towards Standish on Coppull Moor. It was in this area south of Chorley that Thornhagh was mortally wounded.(Photo © JThomas (cc-by-sa/2.0)

On the morning of 18 August, near Chorley, Thornhagh pushed forward too boldly without wearing his full armour, leading the charge of his troops from the front. Scottish lancers were thus able to isolate him and wound him in his body, thigh and head. He was carried, mortally wounded, to the rear of the battle by his soldiers and lived long enough to witness his troops win this encounter. Lucy Hutchinson provides us with a most moving account of this event, no doubt told to her husband Colonel John Hutchinson by Thornhagh's officers:

> But, in the beginning of the battle, the valiant Colonel Thornhagh was wounded to death. Being in the beginning of the charge upon a horse as courageous as became such a master, he made furious speed to set upon a company of Scotch lancers, that he was singly engaged and mortally wounded, before it was possible for his regiment, though as brave men as ever drew sword and too affectionate to their Colonel to be slack in following him, to come time enough to break the fury of that body which shamed not to unite all their force against one man: who fell not among them, but being faint and covered in blood, of his enemies, as his own, was carried off by some of his own men, while the rest, enraged for the loss of their dear Colonel, fought not that day like men of human race; deaf to the cries of every coward that asked mercy, they killed all and would not a captive [should] live to see their Colonel die, but said the whole kingdom of Scotland was too mean a sacrifice for that brave man, whose soul was hovering to take her flight out of his body, but that an eager desire to know the success of that battle kept it within till the end of the day, when the news being brought to him, he cleared his dying countenance and said "I now rejoice to die, since God hath let me see the overthrow of this perfidious enemy; I could not lose my life in a better cause, and I have favour from the Lord to see my blood avenged". So he died, with a large testimony of love to his soldiers, but more to the cause, and was by mercy removed, that the temptations of future times might not prevail to corrupt his pure soul. A man of greater courage and integrity fought not, nor fell not in this glorious cause; he had an excellent good nature, but easy to be wrought upon

> by flatterers, yet as flexible to the admonitions of his friends; and this virtue he had, that if sometimes a cunning insinuation prevailed upon his easy faith, when his error was made known to him, notwithstanding all his great courage, he was readier to acknowledge and repair, than to pursue his mistake.[21]

This was praise indeed, written many years after the event, from a woman not renowned for writing kind words about those who had disagreed with or argued with her husband. Cromwell, in writing his report to the Speaker following his victory, was no less generous in his praise of Colonel Thornhagh:

> I ordered Colonel Thornhagh to command two or three regiments of horse to follow the enemy, if it were possible to make him stand till we could bring up the army … and in this prosecution that worthy gentleman Colonel Thornhagh, pressing too boldly, was slain, being run into the body, and thigh, and head by the enemy's launcers: and give me leave to say he was a man as faithful and gallant in your service as any, and one who often heretofore lost blood in your quarrel, and now his last.[22]

Lucy Hutchinson's account suggests that Thornhagh took several hours to die of his wounds, 'till the end of the day', and the victory reported to him probably one of the many skirmishes that took place prior to the Scottish foot's defeat at Winwick Pass, north of Warrington on 19 August. The Parliamentarian horse, including Thornhagh's regiment, continued to press upon the Scottish forces all the way to Winwick, probably leaving their commander to die on the battlefield with a few troops to support him. Thornhagh was buried on the battlefield near to Chorley at a place called the Red Bank.[23] The place was certainly remembered, for two months later his remains were retrieved and buried at the family church at Sturton le Steeple in Nottinghamshire.

Though bereft of their colonel, the Nottinghamshire horse still had a military duty to perform alongside the other cavalry regiments and this they did with great resolve. It was later claimed that the main body of Cromwell's army that followed the horse saw Scottish corpses by the roadside all the way from Preston to Wigan.[24] By 19 August, Cromwell's main army had caught up with the horse and about midday at Winwick, just south of the township of Newton, the Scottish foot under the command of William Baille made a stand against them. Here the Scots experienced a rout more considerable than that at Preston and what remained of the foot surrendered at Warrington the next day. Thornhagh's regiment, now under the command of Major Saunders, took part in this battle. The Duke of Hamilton with around 3,000 cavalry managed to escape southwards and Cromwell sent his horse in pursuit of them. Finally on 25 August, with his troops hungry, exhausted and almost

21 Keeble, *Lucy Hutchinson*, pp. 224–5.

22 Lomas (ed.), *The Letters and Speeches of Oliver Cromwell*, I, pp. 279–85.

23 <http://www.british-history.ac.uk/vch/lancs/vol6/129–149>, accessed 30 November 2019.

24 Woolrych, *Battles of the English Civil War*, p. 175.

The approximate line of the Scottish infantry deployment at Winwick Bank (Photo © S.Brown (cc-by-sa/2.0)

at the point of mutiny, Hamilton surrendered at Uttoxeter.[25] Cromwell had earned a momentous victory.

After Thornhagh's death on the evening of 18 August, temporary command of his regiment would have passed to its major Thomas Saunders, identified in the 1647 petition submitted to Lord Fairfax. Lucy Hutchinson wrote of him 'Major Saunders (a Derbyshire man who was a very godly, honest, country gentleman, but had not many things requisite to a great soldier) assigned them for their major and with him he brought in about a troop of Derbyshire horse'.[26]

Once the Preston campaign was over, Lucy Hutchinson claimed that the troops in the regiment had clamoured for her husband, Thornhagh's longtime friend, to be appointed commander of the regiment. In the end, Cromwell went on to appoint Saunders as its new colonel. Despite the vitriol of Lucy Hutchinson about this appointment, it made sound military sense. By the end of 1648, the Nottinghamshire horse was no longer just a county unit but a cosmopolitan one as more recruits were brought in from further afield to keep it up to strength. Saunders had been with this regiment for at least 12 months as its major, probably longer, and after Thornhagh's death he had performed well, in Cromwell's opinion, over the remainder of the Preston campaign. The regiment had other military honours to gain after 1648, but it was no longer Thornhagh's regiment or just a Nottinghamshire force.

25 Woolrych, *Battles of the English Civil War,* pp. 176–8.
26 Keeble, *Lucy Hutchinson,* p. 225.

7

Securing the Inheritance

Francis Thornhagh was dead, slain at the battle of Preston, but how that information was conveyed to his young widow and aged mother back in Nottinghamshire remains unclear. Cromwell had written to the House of Commons on 20 August reporting his initial victory at the battle of Preston and this was read to the MPs on 23 August 1648. In that same sitting, the journal recorded 'Ordered, That it be referred to the Committee of the Northern Association, to consider and present some way of Recompense and Satisfaction to be given to the wife and children of Colonel Thornhagh, for his gallant service, who lost his life in this said service against the Scots'.[1]

It is interesting to note that although Thornhagh was then fighting with Cromwell's forces, it was to the Northern Association committee that Parliament referred this case. The Nottinghamshire horse were still considered to be part of that army but had been temporarily seconded to Cromwell. As the regiment was still involved in mopping up operations against the Scots on this date, it is most likely that the news was conveyed personally to Thornhagh's widow by one of the then sitting Nottinghamshire MPs. It possibly fell to his brother-in-law, Gervase Pigott, who was to have an ongoing involvement with Thornhagh's children for the next 20 years, to deliver the bad news. Had it been his close friend John Hutchinson, also a sitting MP at that time, who had undertaken the task it would most certainly have been mentioned in Lucy Hutchinson's memoirs.

The Amended Will of Francis Thornhagh

Depositions regarding the will and a copy of the probate inventory of Francis Thornhagh are all that survive in the archival deposits from this period.[2] What is clear from these surviving sources though, is that there were some questions asked about additions made to the will just before Thornhagh rode off to join up with Cromwell in May 1648. Two individuals made depositions

1 HC Journal, V, 23 August 1648, p. 620.

2 NA, Deposition of Francis Thornhagh, PRNW 7245, 22 September 1648 and Inventory of Francis Thornhagh, esq., 17 November 1648, DD/FJ/4/17/2.

to the court about the veracity of the will. These individuals were John Harrison of Sturton le Steeple and Thomas Mounke of south Leverton. The latter gave a detailed statement about events he witnessed at Thornhagh's home in Nottingham

> This deponent beinge servante to the said Francis Thornhagh deceased, and being in the parlor of the said master's dwelling house in Nottingham with his said master. Ye said Francis Thornhagh about three or foure daies after the date of the saide last Will and Testament (being engaged to go in the business & design against Pembrooke Castle) had in his hande his last will & testament written in parchment & his name subscribed & his Crest sett thereunto, and laying it down upon the table he saide this will make all straight. The saide Francis Thornhagh being then very well and of p'fect mynde and understanding. And this deponent further saith that presently after the saide Francis Thornhagh went up unto the chamber of his wife leaving the said last will and testament behind him upon the table, which this deponent in the mean time perused & read fully, and this deponent saith that the will and testament now handed unto him is the very same will and testament that he then saw and perused and that the condicions therein made, were then soe, when he perused it, and that all things therein contained were so done and written as they now are without any alteracon, addicion or divergence, which this deponent knoweth to be true, because he then looked upon it.[3]

Both deponents were described as yeomen, with Harrison being described as a resident of the parish of Sturton, the family home of the Thornhagh family and Mounke a resident of the adjacent parish of south Leverton. With Francis Thornhagh and his family being based at Nottingham, as his mother retained the home at Fenton as a dower, it was probably the case that both individuals were appointed to manage the lands there for Francis Thornhagh, especially whilst the Colonel was involved with the First Civil war. They may have come over to Nottingham, where the events described above occurred, to receive instructions prior to Thornhagh's departure to the siege at Pembroke Castle. Whilst here they either witnessed the additions or saw the will after they had been made.

The 'condicions' described by Mounke may well have been a codicil attached to the original will. In the absence of the will, it is difficult to be sure of what these were but they almost certainly related to the birth of a son and heir only months previously and possibly the recent death of a daughter, Frances, in her infancy. It is possible that later additions or alterations to the will were either badly annotated, or apparently contradicted something within the earlier text and it was this that the two men were asked to address. Details from the *Visitation of Nottingham* in 1662, clearly record that Gervase Pigott had been appointed the guardian of John Thornhagh (then aged 15) and may well have been guardian also of Francis Thornhagh's daughters

3 NA, Deposition of Thomas Monke within the Deposition of Francis Thornhagh, PRNW 22 September 1648.

during their younger years.[4] In many ways this was a sensible action, for Thornhagh's widow, Elizabeth, was still a young woman and would probably marry again if her husband were killed. In fact, she did not remarry until 1655 when she wed a distant cousin, William Skeffington of Skeffington in the county of Leicester.[5] As she had been a co-heiress with her sister, Gervase Pigott's wife, to her late father's estate in Gotham, Nottinghamshire, Thornhagh needed a trusted guardian to both protect and disentangle the estates should his widow remarry. He chose well with his brother-in-law, as even Lucy Hutchinson felt moved to extol his virtues.

> Mr Pigott was a very religious, serious wise gentleman, true-hearted to God and his country, of a generous and liberal nature, one that thought nothing too dear to expose nor too difficult to undertake for his friend; one that delighted not in the ruin of his neighbours, but could endure rather than the destruction of religion, law and liberty; one that wanted not courage, yet chose rather to venture himself as a single person than as a leader in arms, and to serve his country in counsel than in action, there was no man in his nature and his whole deportment, that approved himself more a gentleman than he.[6]

After the restoration of the monarchy in 1660, such was Pigott's reputation that he endured no sanction for his previous service and even enjoyed the friendship of the antiquarian and avowed Royalist Dr Robert Thoroton.[7] In the surviving Thornhagh family papers there are a number of documents regarding settlement arrangements for the widow Elizabeth Thornhagh, from around the time of her remarriage, all of which are signed or conveyed by Pigott. He also undertook, as guardian to minor John Thornhagh, some land exchanges for the consolidation of the Thornhagh estate.[8] Gervase Pigott appears to have undertaken his responsibility of guardian with great care and consideration and was probably involved in supporting the family in arranging the funeral for Francis Thornhagh's mother, Jane, when she died in January 1661, as her grandson was only 14 at the time and her former daughter-in-law had remarried.

The Probate Inventory of Francis Thornhagh: Snapshots of a Life

Although at his death, Thornhagh was still in the process of claiming back from Parliament expenses amounting to £1,030 incurred in raising his regiment for them, alongside arrears of pay which the treasurers of war had

4 G. D. Squibb (ed.), W. Dugdale, *The Visitation of Nottinghamshire begun in 1662 and finished in 1664* (London: Harleian Society Publications, 1986), p. 29.

5 Ford, *Town on the Street*, p. 37.

6 Keeble, *Lucy Hutchinson*, p. 98.

7 J. Goodall, 'Thrumpton Hall, Nottinghamshire: A treasure on the Trent' in *Country Life*, 5 November 2017.

8 NA, Settlements of widow Elizabeth Thornhagh and Land exchange papers, DD/FJ/3/4/3/4–7.

estimated to be £358. 8s. The inventory of his goods at Nottingham taken in November 1648 shows him to still be a gentleman of considerable means. The inventory of his possessions identifies fifteen rooms in his house; hall, a street and a hall parlour, pantry, kitchen with bolting house, cellar, great chamber, yellow chamber, a matted and a little garret, old gallery, boarded chamber, stair chamber, a little forward chamber and a Castell chamber, whilst in the yard were stables, barn and a brew house. A full transcription of the inventory is provided in Appendix I. Such was the detail within the inventory that the parchment document, though only 15 cm wide, extends for 195 cm.

The total value appraised of all his moveable goods – land and property were not included in the inventory – amounted to £534.15s. The appraisers of Thornhagh's estate were all local men and would have been known to the decease, if not of his immediate circle of friends or business contacts. They clearly put considerable effort into making an accurate list for they acted under solemn oath, and executors, widow, creditors and heirs could challenge their valuations. Moving from room to room they listed furniture, utensils and household goods in each. As Thornhagh's inventory is so detailed it provides a helpful insight into both his living conditions as a gentleman of considerable means and also his domestic arrangements.[9]

Francis Thornhagh's love of horses and horsemanship is reflected in the thirteen horses identified in the stables, and appraised at £87. 6s. They included one grey gelding, two bay geldings, a bay stone horse, one grey mare, two bay and two grey nags (small horses or ponies) and a bay breeding mare and three young ones. Whether the fine mounts he took with him to Pembroke and later Preston, possibly the ones awarded to him by Parliament, had been returned to the stables after his death or just absorbed into the machinery of war to supply dismounted troopers after the battle, remains unclear. The same might also be said of the armour and weapons he took with him on campaign, as the inventory only identifies swords and pistols to the value of £5 and some old muskets and fowling pieces at £3. His continued love of learning, as befitted a gentleman of his status, is reflected in the value placed upon his collection of books in the study at £10.5s. This was higher than the total value of all the weapons listed in the house.

The hall in the house was listed first in the inventory, suggesting it was into this you first entered when coming into the house from the street and as such it contained little furniture. The street parlour, at the front of the house on St Mary's Hill, Nottingham, was probably the room where visitors were entertained for it contained ten chairs covered in leather, two tables, numerous stools, cupboard and three carpets. There were also in the room a picture and two maps on the walls, which were appraised at £2.

The 'Great Chamber' contained one 'couch chayre' (a sofa with an arm or rests at each end), three old chairs, a safe and most moving of all a cradle, possibly for the use of his son who was around 10 months old at the time of the inventory. This may have served as the day room for the lady of the house.

9 D. Hey, *Journeys in Family History* (London: The National Archives, 2004), pp. 211–221.

The two main sleeping chambers appear to have been the Matted Chamber and the Yellow Chamber, as both contained bedsteads with curtains, feather mattresses, valances and bolsters. The colour scheme for the Matted Chamber was green and may have been so called because of the seven pieces of tapestry hung on the walls and valued at £7. Unsurprisingly the colour scheme for the yellow chamber was yellow with curtains and bedding of that colour.

Across all the chambers on the second floor were recorded a large amount of sheets, linen, towels, napkins and cloth. With the Castell Chamber there were a pair of Holland sheets (36s.), three flaxen sheets (30s.), a further four pairs of flaxen sheets (£2.15s.) and 44 yards of old diaper (linen fabric with a diamond pattern weave) and damask cloth (£3.10s.) alongside old sheets, napkins, tablecloths, towels and 'pillowbeeres' which were valued in total at £6.15s. Also stored, possibly in the same chamber, was one set of green curtains and valance (£3.10s), taffeta (possibly silk) twist (£5), a canopy bed (£2.10s.) and a further 'six pieces of hangings' appraised at £12.

Much of the produce of the Thornhagh lands at Fenton appears to have been stored in the out buildings of their Nottingham house. Malt and barley to the value of £22 alongside hay at £18 were noted in the barns. Four cows, for milking, valued at £18, nine swine hogs, turkeys, ducks and hens were also recorded and assessed at 20s. The servants produced cheese and beer at the house for in the brew house were noted a cheese press and brewing vessels whilst in the little garret were sixty-three small cheeses.

In spite of the fact that the town of Nottingham had been attacked and entered several times over the years 1643–1645, Thornhagh had managed to retain £58 worth of plate within his home. He possibly had a secret hiding place where his valuables were hidden in case of such contingencies and there was also recorded the presence of a safe in the great chamber. By far the most valuable possessions, in monetary terms, was his 'purse and apparel' which were appraised at £150, which was just over 28 percent of the total value of the inventory. Unfortunately individual items were not recorded under this category, so the divide between coins and attire is not listed.

The sheer number of possessions recorded in the house conveys to the reader a sense of the wealth of the Thornhagh family at the death of Francis, at the relatively young age of just under 31.

After Francis Thornhagh's Death

As soon as the executors of the will of Francis gained permission from the court to proceed with implementing the will, one of the first things they set about doing was retrieving the Colonel's body from his battlefield burial. Exactly two months after his death in action, the registers of Sturton le Steeple parish church record the burial of Francis's body in the chancel on 18 October 1648. He was buried at the feet of his father, Sir Francis Thornhagh, who had been buried in the chancel five years earlier on 1 May 1643. Originally both had been given table tombs near the north and south walls of the chancel but in 1870 these had been removed and the slabs only were replaced on the floor at the same spots. Colonel Francis Thornhagh's slab is engraved with

the Thornhagh family coat of arms and bears an inscription in Latin around the edges. This translates as follows:

> What remains of Francis Thornhagh Esquire, Colonel of a company of cavalry is lying here, who, exposed to many dangers, passed to his rest on the 18th August in the seventh year of this most terrible war, in the 31st year of his age, the year of Christ 1648. He left offspring by his most excellent wife, Elizabeth St Andrea [Andrew], John, Elizabeth, Jane.[10]

Facing page: the gravestone of Colonel Francis Thornhagh in Sturton-le-Steeple church in Nottinghamshire. (Author's photo)

A full and active life tragically cut short but summed up in such a simple but moving epitaph.

The family remained in their Nottingham home, with Thornhagh's widow enjoying the support of her sister and brother-in-law and many friends, including that of Lucy and John Hutchinson. They were also conveniently placed to monitor the estate at Fenton and also near to John's grandmother, the dowager Jane, who was still living in the family home there. Possibly John, like his father Francis, was sent as a boarder for his education at around the age of eight, and in 1664 he was admitted to Jesus College, Cambridge at the age of 16. It appears that the family remained at the Nottingham house, which was left to John on reaching an age of maturity (in the absence of the will it is difficult to ascertain how this was specified), even after his mother remarried in 1655. According to the historian Robert Thoroton 'William Skeffington, Esquire and Elizabeth his wife, the relict of Francis Thornhagh, resided in this Town in an House on St Mary Hill, purchased of Thomas Mucklow of Broughton Sulney'.[11]

By the time of the 1674 Hearth Tax returns – the 1664 returns do not survive for Nottingham – William and Elizabeth were no longer living in Nottingham, suggesting that the house and inheritance had now come to John and they were free to move to Leicestershire to start their new home together. This may in fact have happened as early as 1666, considering the two sisters of John were six and four years older than him.

The Thornhagh family's long links with both Sturton and Nottingham continued long after the devastating death of Colonel Francis Thornhagh. Under the son John (1648–1723) the family's financial situation improved considerably and the estate was expanded. He followed in his father's footsteps serving as High Sheriff of Nottingham (1688–89) and MP for Retford (1689–1702) and Nottinghamshire (1704–1710). In 1678, John sold his Nottingham residence and purchased the manor of Osberton in Nottinghamshire. He retained the estate at Fenton but the family now established themselves at the new house, leaving the old manor house at Fenton to gradually fall into ruin.[12] Although the paternal line of the family came to an end in 1787, members of the family through the maternal line continue to live in and around Osberton even today and remain, rightly so, proud of their ancestor's deeds across the period of the British Civil Wars.

10 Ford, *Town on the Street*, p. 69.

11 J. Throsby (ed.), *Thoroton's History of Nottingham, Republished with Large Additions by John Throsby*, 3 vols (Nottingham: John Throsby, 1790–96), II, Section III, pp. 34–70.

12 Ford, *Town on the Street*, 37–38.

Conclusion

Internal evidence within Lucy Hutchinson's *Memoirs of the Life of Colonel Hutchinson*, suggests that she completed the manuscript for her family's private use between the year of her husband's death in 1664 and 1671. Within her account she mentions two officers who served under Colonel Thornhagh, John Wright and Richard Frank, both of whom were arrested at the same time as John Hutchinson in 1663 and were taken to Newark to be held. In her manuscript she continues 'where they are yet prisoners, and to this day know not why'.[1] According to Thomas Bailey in his *Annals of Nottingham* (1835) and also later historians, Captain John Wright was released from jail at the Assizes on 7 July 1671, suggesting that the *Memoirs* were completed by this date.[2]

Looking back, therefore, over 20 years to the death of Colonel Thornhagh, Lucy Hutchinson wrote of his death with an emotional intensity that had not diminished over the years. At the end of her account of events at Preston she makes the candid observation that Thornhagh was 'by mercy removed, that the temptations of future times might not prevail to corrupt his pure soul'.[3] For the Colonel's family his death would have come as an immediate personal disaster, but ironically subsequent events immediately after 1648 meant that at the Restoration of Charles II in 1660, the Thornhagh's incurred none of the penalties or stigma that other prominent Parliamentarian families had to endure. When Charles I was beheaded in 1649, the heir to the family estate was just a year old and his father, the Colonel, had been dead for over six months so therefore had taken no part in the trial or execution of the King.

Colonel Francis Thornhagh's reputation as a brave and good officer of soldiers, held so highly over his lifetime, was subsequently overshadowed by the events of the republic and a further succession of military successes by Cromwell, Ireton and others. Though his achievements were never completely forgotten, they have been increasingly overlooked over time, with the return of the monarchy in 1660 further aiding the process. Not until the start of the nineteenth century was there a major renewal of interest in the exploits and achievements of some of the local Nottinghamshire Parliamentarian officers

1 Keeble, *Lucy Hutchinson*, p. 298.

2 T. Bailey, *Annals of Nottinghamshire*, 4 Vols (London: Simpkin, Marshall & co, 1853), entry for year 1671. See also P. R. Seddon, 'The dating of the completion of the composition of the Memoirs of Colonel John Hutchinson: the evidence of Captain John Wright and Lieutenant Richard Franck', *TTS,* 120 (2016), pp. 113–20.

3 Keeble, *Lucy Hutchinson*, p. 225.

and supporters. The publication by the Reverend Julius Hutchinson in 1806 of Lucy Hutchinson's manuscript *Memoirs* stimulated this process greatly. Yet, even though Thornhagh figured both prominently and positively in her recollections, more so than any other figure bar John Hutchinson himself, it did little to encourage further research into his life and exploits. Over the next 200 years only a well-researched, but brief, academic paper on his life by Professor Alfred Wood was never published and Thornhagh himself even failed to warrant an entry in the *Dictionary of National Biography*.

The question might be asked whether this would have been any different had he not been killed at Preston in 1648? Given that many of Thornhagh's closest friends and comrades, including John Hutchinson, Gilbert Millington, Henry Ireton and Oliver Cromwell and two other Nottinghamshire individuals not unknown to him, Edward Whalley and Francis Hacker, were heavily involved in the trial and execution of the 'man of blood', Charles I, it is extremely unlikely that the Colonel would have remained aloof from these events. Thornhagh's role as an MP between 1646–48 would have opened his eyes to the duplicity of the King in his dealings with the different factions. His service as a soldier in 1648, seeing the bloodshed in action at Wales and at the battle of Preston as a result of Charles' machinations, would also have impacted upon him. As has been displayed throughout this biography, Thornhagh was a man who 'wore his heart on his sleeve' and he would have probably been caught up with the angst expressed by the army following the ending of the Second Civil War. It is not impossible that he too may have become one of the Regicides, creating for him notoriety and all sorts of other subsequent problems for his family and the estate at the restoration of the monarchy.

Lucy Hutchinson was probably right in her assessment of the fortunate timing of his death, whilst in no way diminishing the personal impact of it upon his family. Yet to his friends and comrades in arms, from Cromwell down to his loyal troops, Francis Thornhagh was and remained a 'gallant and worthy gentleman' who died fighting for a cause which he greatly believed in. His short and active life added lustre to the already rising reputation of the Thornhagh family name and his death at Preston left his son with the opportunity to re-establish the family's fortunes and status within the shire, and at Parliament, once he reached his age of maturity. Francis Thornhagh's choice of Gervase Pigott as guardian for his son and the resolve and determination of his wife Elizabeth and his mother the dowager Jane, held the family and the estate together over the turbulent decade of the 1650s.

Maybe the last word on Colonel Francis Thornhagh should be left to a local antiquarian of that time. Dr Robert Thoroton wrote a history of Nottinghamshire published in 1677 and his Royalist credentials can be clearly discerned in his comments (or lack thereof) about former Parliamentarians. Of Thornhagh though, he wrote more positively: 'He was a valiant man, and a colonel of horse for the Parliament, in whose service he lost his life by a Scotch lance, as it was said at the battle begun near Preston in Lancashire, between duke Hamilton and that party'.[4]

4 Throsby, III, p.296.

Appendix I

Inventory of Goods of the Late Francis Thornhagh of Nottingham, Esq.

17 November 1648
Nottinghamshire Archives
DD/FJ/4/17/2

(original spellings retained)

A True and Perfect Inventory
of all and singular the goods and chattels
of Francis Thornhagh late of the
Towne & County of the towne of
Nottingham Esquire deceased. Taken &
Praysed by Thomas Malin, Richard
Cowlishawe and George Allseabrook
the seaventeenth daie of November Anno
Domi 1648. As followth: viz

Imprimis in the Hall two tables and two formes and eight peeces of seeling and one small trunke	£3.	10s.
Item. Within the Street Parlor Eight lay irons, eight coused stooles And two lowe stooles		38s.
Item. Ten chayres covered with leather	£2.	
Item. One small table and two side tables	£2.	

Item. One cubbard and three carpets	£2.	6s.	8d.
Item. One picture & two Mapps	£2.		
Item. One fire shovel and Tongues one case of knives and one paire of snuffers with one small Grate		5s.	
Item. Within the Parlor Clossett potts and glasses, two paper bookes, juggs, boxes and shelves		20s.	
Item. Within the hall Parlor two lowe bedsteads & one Feather bed, one flockbed, two coverlids, one rug, two blankets, one great Chest and a trunke, three bolsters one little table and a spade and two paire of Fetters	£4.		
Item. Within the Pantry one presse for lynnings, two wheeles two casements and old glasses one Lambe skyn and a paire of blades & a Table cover	13s.	4d.	
Item. Within the Brewhouse fore coales, one cheese presse and brewing vessels	£3.	5s.	
Item. Within the kitchen, one racke, seaven pans, two skelletts, fower potts, two dripping panns, three spits, one fire shovel & tongs, one paire of racks, one brasse morter & pestle, one brasse saucer, three little ladles and the gally balkes, and five hookes, one frying panne, two paire of Pott hookes	£6.		
Item. One table, two chayres, Fower stooles, two wheeles, two Reeles, one leather Jacke with other milking vessels and Tyn plates and Ticknall vessels & one flicke of Bacon, one close			

stoole, panes, dishes and trenchers one grate & one brandyiron		33s.	4d.
Item. Within the bolting house	6s.		
Item. Within the sellar, one Hogshead with some empty Vessels and for salte butter & A thrall and a frame		30s.	
Item. Fore pewter dishes, flagons, Spoones, porringers & chamber pottes and plates	£2.	4s.	
Item. More pewter seates and a paire of tables	£2.		
Item. Within the great chamber, one couch chayre, three old chayres & ten chayre frames and ten stoole frames and one resting stoole frame, one [crone] frame and a safe, one cradle and five curten rodds and haire lyme	£3.		
Item. Within the matted chamber, one bedstead with greene curtens and vallens laced, and one quilte, fower blankets, fower pillows, one boulster, one Feather bed and matt, and three greene laced chayres	£10.		
Item. One seeing glasse & one old chaire, one stoole, oe foote stoole, one little table, one chamber pott and one Bason		10s.	
Item. Seaven peeces of Tapestry worke	£7.		
Item. Within the Yellowe Chamber, one bedstead with yellow curtaines and valance, one Feather bed and bolster, two pillows, three blankets, one			

wrought cubbard cloath with curten rodds and a Matt, one table, one chaire, fower old hangings, two old peeces of matt, one old fire Iron	£5.	
Item. Within the matted Garrett, one bedstead with white wrought curtens and vallens, one red rug, three blankets and a feather bed, one boulster, two pillows, one mattrice, one matt, three curten rodds, one couch chaire, one cubbord, one stoole and one little fire iron	£7.	
Item. Within the Little Garrett one trundle bed, wheat, Rye & barley, one seeled bed & head three planks, two stooles, frames and Ash balls, one [siph], sixty three small cheeses, one old canopye with curtens	£5.	
Item. All within the old gallery		20s.
Item. Within the space, one chest and a Box		10s.
Item. Within the boarded chamber, one bedstead with curtens and valance, one downe bed, five pillows, one boulster, one greene rug, three blankets, one mattris and a matt	£7.	
Item. Two chayres, three stooles and a stoole frame, six little boxes, two cases, one little Truncke, one little cubbard, one side table, one paire of {hampers) covered with leather, one seeing glasse, two brushes & one little carpet and window curten one fire shovel and tongues, one warming panne and bellowes one paire of snuffers and two smoothing irons	£3.	

Item. Within one little forward chamber, two lowe bedsteads, two feather beds, two matts, six blancketts, three coverings two boulsters, three pillows, one stoole, one bedstoole		£7.	
Item. Within the stare chamber, six pound of teares fowerteene punde of hempe teare, eight pounde of Flaxen yarne, one voyder and a knife, eight dozen of trenchers, two shelves, six pounds of candles, six pounds of sope, two pounds of hopps with barrels and boxes & some other small things		£3.	10s.
Item. For mault and Barley		£22.	
Item. One strike, one shovel & sixty eight sacks and bags			10s.
Item. Within the castell chamber one paire of Holland sheetes			36s.
Item. Three Flaxon sheetes			30s.
Item. Fower paire of Flaxen sheetes	£2.	15s.	
Item. Forty fower yards of old diaper and damaske		£3.	10s.
Item. Fower dozen of old diaper & damaske napkins, one towel and two diaper and damaske napkins		£2.	
Item. Nyne dozen of old flaxen napkins		£2.	10s.
Item. Thirty fower yards of old lynen table clothes			30s.
Item. Six narrow towels			5s.
Item. Seaven wrought pillow beeres		£2.	10s.

Item. Six paire of old Holland pillow beeres and eleaven old flaxon pillowbeeres		25s.
Item. Five paires of old course sheetes and three course table clothes		25s.
Item. Three Elles of Holland & fower yards of harden		10s.
Item. One sett of greene curtens and valence	£3.	10s.
Item. One Taffatie twiste	£5.	
Item. Thirty yards of flannell And canvis		20s.
Item. Six peeces of hangings	£12.	
Item. For a canopie bed	£2.	10s.
Item. Fower candlesticks		5s.
Item. Twenty yards of harden		10s.
Item. Two dozen and a halfe of napkins & five little towels		10s.
Item. Ten paire of old shettes	£2.	8s.
Item. Two diaper table cloathes		10s.
Item. Six yards of tufted Fustian		5s.
Item. Three paire of Flaxon sheetes		30s.
Item. Fower little table cloathes		12s.
Item. Six pillowbeeres, one napkin and a towel		8s.
Item. Fower truncks, one chest and a box		20s.
Item. For tymber in the yard	£3.	

Item. For playster & coales, one carte, one stone trough and other broad stones, two wheele barrowes and a thrall, one old wheele		£3.	10s.
Item. Three ladders, pickforkes and shovels			8s.
Item. Nyne swine hoggs, turkeys, ducks and henns			20s.
Item. Hay within the barne		£18.	
Item. Within the stables. One bay stone horse and baye gelding & one gray gelding		£35.	
Item, One bay bald breeding Mare and three young ones		£25.	
Item. One other baye gelding		£3.	6s.
Item. Two bay nags, two gray nags and one grey mare		£24.	
Item. Fower cowes		£18.	
Item. Saddles, Bridles and two Port mantles		£5.	
Item. Swords and pistols		£5.	
Item. Old muskets & fowling peeces			£3.
Item. The Bookes in the study	£10.	5s.	
Item. In plate		£58.	
Item. His purse & Apparrell		£150.	
Summa totalis		**£534.**	**15s.**

Appendix II

Troopers and Officers Identified as Having Served in the Nottinghamshire Horse under Colonel Thornhagh's Command

Sources identified in [ ] brackets

Lieutenant Colonel	
George Hutchinson	Nottingham [Hough, Hutchinson]
Majors	
Henry Ireton	Transferred to Oliver Cromwell's regiment after the battle of Gainsborough in July 1643 [Hutchinson]
( ) Meldrum	[Hough]
Thomas Saunders	Took command of regiment after Thornhagh's death [Firth]
Captains	
( ) Barrett	[Hough]
Henry Champion	North Collingham [Hough, Wood]
Richard Creed	[Firth]
William Hall	[Hough]
Edward Nethercotes	Dragoon, killed in action [Petition]
George Palmer	Possibly cornet promoted to captain (Firth)
Laurence Palmer	[Hough]
Barry/Philip Pendock	Tollerton [Hough, Wood, Firth]

Thomas Selbie	[Hough]
Charles White	of Newthorpe [Hough, Wood] [Hough]
John Wright	Nottingham [Petition and Wood]
Quartermaster	
Richard Franck	1647, Lieutenant in 1658 (Firth)
Troopers	
Thomas Collishaw	Bilborough. At battle of Gainsborough and Assault of Lincoln (1643) Captured at Newark and held prisoner for 36 weeks [Petition]
Richard Cooper	Received pension for wounds [Petition]
Richard Farnsworth	Killed at battle of Trent Bridge [Petition]
Richard Taylor	Wounded at third siege of Newark [Petition]
( ) Webster	Sheffield(?) Killed at Shelford in 1645 [Petition]

Sources

Hough PRO, Accounts of John Hough SP 28/174.

Firth Firth, Sir C. & Davies, G. *The Regimental History of Cromwell's Army*, 2 Vols (Oxford: Clarendon Press, 1940).

Petition <http://www.civilwarpetitions.ac.uk>

Wood A .C. Wood, *Nottinghamshire in the Civil War* (East Ardsley: S. R. Publishers, 1971).

Appendix III

The Examination of Captain George Palmer Taken Before the Committee at Leicester, 30th March 1644[1]

March 30th 1644, 1644 – George Palmer, Captain Lieutenant to Colonell Thornhagh, examined, sayth that upon Saterday, the 16th of March instant, this examinant commanded the forlorne hope wch was sent out by Order from Sir Edward Hartopp against the enemies then being about Mountsorrell, wch order was to that effect:

That the examinant with the forlorne hope should goe to a certaine hill neere to Mountsorrell, there to make a stand until the rest of the body of the pliament side come up; whereupon the enemye beinge betwixt the hill & this examinant, this examinant seeing the enemie plunderinge horses from the plowmen in the field, there fell upon them, tooke three prisoners and forcd the other backe, and soe came to the hill. Then Sir Edward sent word to this examinant that he went too fast for the bodie to followe, and this examinant, hearinge by Scouts sent before that the enemye was squandered and dispiersed in the towne, went on and pursued the enemye.

Then Sir Edward sent againe to make a stand, wch this examinant did. Then the examinants scouts cominge in brought intelligence, and likewise this examinant hearde by some townsmen of Mountsorrell and others that the enemye was in their quarters in divers townes thereabouts, and divers of their foote dranke in Mountsorrell, whereupon this examinant sent Sir Edward notice thereof, desiringe to knowe whether he should fall on or not, and desiringe some asystance from him; but this Examinant was Comanded by Captayne Innis in Sir Edwards name to march hard by the townes side and there to stand; then the Enemye, perceiving their Comminge, drewe as

1 Public Record Office (now National Archives), State Papers Domestic, Charles I, vol. 501, paper 56.

manye as they could get together for the present into Battalia to face them in the meadowe betwixt them and the Enemye.

Then, by Order of Capt. Ennys, this Examinant charged the enemye with the forlorne hope, and forced them to retreat over a bridge; and, the enemy facing about, the forlorne hope rid forciblye over the bridge, and forced them backe into Mountsorrell. Then Sir Edward Hartopp, cominge up wth the bodie, stood looking upon the forlorne hope, but would sende them noe reliefe, although sent to for it; wch the Enemye perceiving sent reliefe to their bodye and soe beat this Examinant and the forlorne hope backe; whereat the troops of Collonel Thornhays regiment were ready to mutinye upon sight thereof, and sayd they would not suffer this Examinant to be soe ingaged in their sight. Then came up a Lincolnshire troop without Order, as they sayd to relieve this Examinant, when they were beaten backe by the enemy into the towne; but being yet too weake, the enemy, seeing noe more helpe come, cut of divers of the forlorne hope and tooke manie prisoners and rescued their men prisoners taken from them, wch were considerable for number and qualitie.

Then this Examinant, being tyred in fight, went to Sr Edward and desired some reliefe, telling him their extremitye; but he answered this Examinant asking what authoritye this Examinant had to goe over the bridge into the towne, and told this examinant that a counsel of warre should goe on him and them yt seconded him; then this Examinant, urging him for a fresh horse, he sayd he had none for this Examinant, whereupon this Examinant told Major Sanders thereof, who much grieved thereat helped this examinant to a fresh horse, wherewith this Examinant cominge to Sir Edward for Orders, he Comanded all should retyre. Yet notwithstanding, this Examinant wth a Company of dragoons charged the enemye againe into the towne, and so brought most of his men and kept the towne. Then Sir Edward sent Order againe that all the horse & dragoons should retire agayne, although they were very secure, being baracadoed wth Carts in the towne; and soe they left it with great store of provisions of the enemyes wch they had taken from them, whereby they lost their quarter and provisions there & were forced to be all night without provision for horse or man.

The next daye, being Saboath daye, some of the Nottingham troopes told Sir Edward in the Examinant's hearinge yt if he would not suffer them to fight they would goe home. Who answered that he had no Comission to fight, and if their Collonel was there he woulde hange up some of them for being soe forward, and soe passed from them. The next daye, when the fight was at Cotes bridge, and the foote ingaged in fight wth the enemye, this Examinant went to Sir Edward for Orders to assist them, but Sir Edward sent this Examinant & Nottingham troops to the toppe of Stanford hill, there to stand until further Order from him wch they had none until they were commanded to retire after the fight was done.

GEORGE PALMER

This examynation was taken before us, and is offered to be justified by the oathe of the Examinate.

Tho. Babington
Tho. Hesilrige
Fr. Smalley
Will Stanley

Appendix IV

Chronology of the Nottinghamshire Horse After the Death of Colonel Thornhagh

1648		Thomas Saunders appointed colonel of regiment and Richard Creed of Warwickshire appointed major
1649	May	Regiment appointed to guard Parliament
	September	The six troops of the regiment are dispersed and quartered at Warwick, Salop, Stafford, Cheshire, Derby and north Wales
1650	End of	Part of regiment in London again
1651	August	Serving with Major General Harrison in Yorkshire
1652		Regiment sent to Scotland
1653	November	Troops of Major Creed, Captain Philip Prime and Captain John Coulson sent back to England
1654	February	Troops of Colonel Saunders, Captain George Palmer and Captain Robert Hope sent back to England
	April	Regiment in Midlands arresting Royalist conspirators
	16 December	Colonel Saunders resigns after Petition of Three Colonels (he was one of the three) disagreeing with the constitution of the Protectorate
1655	May/June	Colonel William Goffe appointed commander of the Nottinghamshire horse
1656		Regiment in the Midlands
1657	December	Richard Cromwell replaces Goffe as colonel of the regiment
1658	March	Regiment ordered back to Scotland
1659	4 July	Major Creed's troop sent to York and two other troop of the Nottinghamshire horse moved nearer to the border in anticipation of Royalist uprising

	October	Major Ralph Knight promoted to Colonel of the regiment
	December	One troop of Nottinghamshire horse protest against Monck's actions and so are dismounted and sent back to England. Here they join up with Major General Lambert's forces and are placed under the command of Captain James Wright. Another Nottinghamshire officer, Lieutenant Franck, is also part of Lambert's army.
1660	January	Nottinghamshire horse march into England with Monck
	February	Regiment quartered in London
	29 May	Regiment drawn up on Blackheath to welcome the King
	December	The Nottinghamshire horse are disbanded by order of Parliament, one of the last regiments to be dismissed.

Source: C. Firth and G. Davies, *The Regimental History of Cromwell's Army*, 2 vols (Oxford: Clarendon Press, 1940), I, pp.277–90.

Bibliography

Primary Manuscript Sources

British Library

Add. MS 16730, Plans of fortified towns and battlefields in England

Add. MS 30305, Fairfax Family Correspondence, 1518–1700

Add. MS 37344, Whitelocke's Annals

E1 (1)–E1920 (3), Thomason Tracts [individual items referenced in footnotes]

Harley MSS 164–6, Sir Simonds D'Ewes' parliamentary diary, 1642–5 transcribed by YCPH

Harley MS 6390, Fairfax Actions in the Civil War

National Archives (NA) Formerly the Public Record Office (PRO)

SP 28/1–120, Army Pay and Supply Warrants, 1624–51

SP 28/174, Accounts of John Hough of Nottingham

SP 28/174 ff.82–89, Parliamentarian Accounts for Broxtowe Hall

SP 28/240, Nottingham County Committee Treasurers Accounts, 1645–1648

Nottinghamshire Archives Office

PRNW 7245, 22 September 1648 Deposition of Francis Thornhagh

DD/HO/18/2, East Retford Parliamentary Election Returns, 1646

DD/FJ, Foljambe Papers

DD/FJ/4/17/1, Inquisition Post Mortem of John Thornhagh of Fenton, Esq. 23 March 1614

DD/FJ/4/17/2, Inventory of Francis Thornhagh, Esq.

DD/FJ/3/4/3/4-7,Settlements of widow Elizabeth Thornhagh

PR, 2021, Parish Registers of St Marys, Nottingham

PR, 3630, Parish Registers of St Peters, Nottingham

Nottingham University Manuscripts Department

A24, Archdeaconry of Nottingham Act Book

DC/NW/3/1/1, Newark Borough Council Minutes, 1600–62

Ne A 98, Account Papers relating to the estates of the Duke of Newcastle. Warrant of Major Charles White

Printed and Digitised Primary Sources

AHRC Project (2017–2021), 'Conflict, Welfare and Memory during and after the English Civil Wars, 1642–1710 at <www.civilwarpetitions.ac.uk>

Baker, W. T. B. (ed.), *Records of the Borough of Nottingham, 1625–1702* (Nottingham: Nottingham Corporation, 1900)

Bennett, M., *A Nottinghamshire Village in War and Peace: The Accounts of the Constables of Upton, 1640–1666* (Nottingham: Thoroton Society, 1995)

Calendar of State Papers Domestic, Charles I (London: HMSO, 1897)

Cavendish, M., ed. C. H. Firth, *The Life of William Cavendish, Duke of Newcastle* (London: G. Routledge & Sons, 1890)

Clarendon, Earl of, ed. W. Dunn Mackay, *The History of the Rebellion and Civil Wars in England*

Copnall, H. Hampton, *Nottinghamshire County Records of the 17th Century* (Nottingham: Henry Saxton, 1915)

Fairfax Correspondence, ed. Robert Bell, vols 3 and 4 (London: Richard Bentley, 1849)

Firth, C. H. (ed.), *Memoirs of the Life of Colonel Hutchinson by his widow Lucy* (London: Routledge, 1906)

Firth, C. H. and Rait, R. S. (eds), *Acts and Ordinances of the Interregnum, 1642–1660* (London: HMSO, 1911)

Firth, J. B., *Highways & Byways in Nottinghamshire* (London: Macmillan & Co., 1924)

Gardiner, S. R., *The Constitutional Documents of the Puritan Revolution* (Oxford, Clarendon Press, 1979, first published 1889)

Keeble, N. H. (ed.), Hutchinson, L., *Memoirs of the Life of Colonel Hutchinson* (London: J. Dent, 1995)

House of Commons Journal, vols 3–7, 1640–53 (London: HMSO, 1802)

House of Lords Journal, vols 5–10, 1640–49 (London: HMSO, 1767–1830)

Kenyon, J. P., *The Stuart Constitution* (Cambridge: Cambridge University Press, 1966)

Rushworth, John, *Historical Collections,* 7 vols (London: D. Browne, 1742)

Squibb, L. V. O. (ed.), Dugdale, W., *The Visitation of Nottinghamshire begun in 1662 and finished in 1664* (London: Harleian Society, 1986)

Thomas, S. C. (ed.), *The Letters and Speeches of Oliver Cromwell with Elucidations by Thomas Carlyle*, 3 vols (London: Methuen & Co., 1904)

Train, K. S. S. (ed.), *Nottinghamshire Visitations, 1662–1664* (Nottingham: Thoroton Society, 1950)

Webster, W. F. (ed.), *Protestation Returns 1641/2, Nottinghamshire and Derby* (Nottingham, 1980)

Webster, W. F. (ed.), *Nottinghamshire Hearth Tax Returns, 1664:1674* (Nottingham: Thoroton Society, 1986)

Whitelock, B., *Memorials of English Affairs from the Beginning of the Reign of Charles I to the Restoration of Charles II* (Oxford: Oxford University Press, 1853)

Wing, D., *Short Title Catalogue of Books ... 1641–1700*, 4 vols (2nd edn, New York: Modern Language Association of America 1998)

Secondary Sources

Books

Adair, J., *By the Sword Divided: Eyewitnesses to the English Civil War* (London: Century Press, 1983)

Appleby, D. J. and Hopper, A. (eds), *Battle-scarred: Mortality, medical care and military welfare in the British Civil Wars* (Manchester: Manchester University Press, 2018)

Aston, R., *The English Civil War: Conservatism and Revolution, 1603–1649* (London: Phoenix, 1997; originally published in 1978)

Aylmer, G. E., and Morrill, J. S., *The Civil War and Interregnum: Sources for Local Historians* (London: Bedford Square Press, 1979)

Bailey, T., *Annals of Nottinghamshire*, 4 vols (London: Simpkin, Marshall & Co, 1853)

Barratt, J., *The Great Siege of Chester* (Stroud: Tempus, 2003)

Beckett, J. (ed.), *A Centenary History of Nottingham* (Manchester: Manchester University Press, 1997)

Bennett, M., *The Civil Wars in Britain and Ireland, 1638–1651* (Oxford: Blackwell, 1997)

Bennett, M., ed., *Society, Religion and Culture in Seventeenth-Century Nottinghamshire* (Lampeter: The Edwin Mellen Press, 2005)

Bennett, M., *Cromwell at War: The Lord General and his Military Revolution* (London: I. B. Tauris, 2017)

Blackmore, D., *Arms and Armour of the English Civil Wars* (London: Royal Armouries, 1990)

Braddick, M., *God's Fury, England's Fire: A New History of the English Civil Wars* (London: Penguin, 2009)

Briggs, A., *A Social History of England* (London: Penguin, 1985)

Bristow, J., *The Local Historian's Glossary & Vade Mecum* (Nottingham: University of Nottingham, 1994), 2nd edn

Brown, C., *A History of Nottinghamshire* (London: Elliot Stock, 1891)

Brown, C., A *History of Newark-on-Trent*, 2 Vols (Nottingham: Nottinghamshire County Council, 1995; originally published 1904)

Bull, S., *Bloody Preston: Battle of Preston 1648* (Lancaster: Carnegie Publishing, 1997)

Cantor, L., *The Changing English Countryside, 1400–1700* (London: Routledge & Kegan, 1987)

Carlton, C., *Going to the Wars: The Experience of the English Civil Wars, 1638–1651* (London: Routledge, 1992)

Clark, P. and Slack, P., *English Towns in Transition, 1500–1700* (Oxford: Oxford University Press, 1976)

Cooke, D., *The Civil War in Yorkshire, Fairfax versus Newcastle* (Barnsley: Pen and Sword, 2004)

Cooke, D., *Yorkshire Sieges of the Civil Wars* (Barnsley: Pen and Sword, 2011)

Coward, B. (ed.), *A Companion to Stuart Britain* (Oxford: Blackwell, 2003)

Coward, B., *The Stuart Age: England, 1603–1714* (Harlow: Pearson Education, 2012, 4th edn)

Cust, R. and Hughes, A. (eds.), *The English Civil War* (London: Arnold, 1997)

Dowen, K., *Arms and Armour of the English Civil Wars* (Leeds: Royal Armouries, 2019)

Edwards, Peter, *Dealing in Death: The Arms Trade and the British Civil Wars, 1638–1651*(Stroud: Sutton, 2000)

Firth, C. H., *Cromwell's Army* (London: Methuen, 1921, 3rd edn)

Firth, Sir C. and Davies, G., *The Regimental History of Cromwell's Army*, 2 vols (Oxford: Clarendon Press, 1940)

Ford, John, *The Town on the Street: The Story of the Nottinghamshire Village of Sturton-Le-Steeple* (Retford: Self Published, 1975)

Gardiner, S. R., *History of the Great Civil War, 1642–9*, 4 vols (Moreton-in-Marsh: Windrush Press, 1991, originally published 1893)

Gaunt, P., *The Cromwellian Gazetteer; An Illustrated Guide to Britain in the Civil War and Commonwealth* (Stroud: Alan Sutton Publishing, 1987)

Gaunt, P., *A Nation under Siege: The Civil War in Wales, 1642–48* (London: HMSO for Cadw, 1991)

Gaunt, P., *Oliver Cromwell* (Oxford: Blackwell, 1996)

Gaunt, P., *The English Civil War: A Military History* (London: I. B. Tauris, 2014)

Gentles, I., *The English Revolution and the Wars in the Three Kingdoms, 1638–1652* (Harlow: Pearson Education, 2007)

Gittings, C., *Death, Burial and the Individual in Early Modern England* (London: Routledge, 1988)

Gurnham, R., *A History of Lincoln* (Chichester: Phillimore, 2009)

Gurnham, R., *A History of Nottingham* (Andover: Phillimore & Co., 2010)

Harrington, P., *English Civil War Archaeology* (London: B. T. Batsford, 2004)

Heal, F. and Holmes, C., *The Gentry in England and Wales, 1500–1700* (Basingstoke: Palgrave, 1994)

Hey, D., *Journeys in Family History* (London: National Archives, 2004)

Hill, C., *The Century of Revolution* (London: Routledge, 1980, 2nd edn)

Hill, Sir F., *Tudor and Stuart Lincoln* (Cambridge: Cambridge University Press, 1956)

Houlbrooke, R., *Death, Religion and the Family in England, 1480–1750* (Oxford: Clarendon Press, 1998)

Houston, R. A., *The Population History of Britain and Ireland* (Cambridge: Cambridge University Press, 1995)

Hughes, A., *The Causes of the English Civil War* (London: Macmillan Press, 1998, 2nd edn)

Hunt, T., *The English Civil War at First Hand* (London: Phoenix, 2002)

Hutton, R., *The Royalist War Effort, 1642–1646* (London: Routledge, 1999)

Ingham, S., *Discovering the Civil War in Nottinghamshire* (Nottingham: Nottinghamshire County Council, 1992)

Jennings, Stuart B., *These Uncertaine Tymes: Newark and the Civilian Experience of the Civil Wars, 1640–1660* (Nottingham: Nottinghamshire County Council, 2009)

Kenyon, J., *The Civil Wars of England* (London; Weidenfeld and Nicolson, 1988)

Kenyon, J. and Ohlmeyer, J. (eds), *The Civil Wars: A Military History of England, Scotland and Ireland, 1638–1660* (Oxford: Oxford University Press, 1998)

Laslett, P., *The World we have Lost, further explored* (London: Routledge, 1983, 3rd edn)

Liddard, C., *Castles in Context, Power, Symbolism and Landscape, 1066–1500* (Macclesfield: Windgathering Press, 2005)

Lindley, K., *The English Civil War and Revolution: A Sourcebook* (London: Routledge, 1998)

Macinnes, A. I., *The British Revolution, 1629–1660* (Basingstoke: Palgrave Macmillan, 2005)

Marcombe, D., *English Small Town Life: Retford, 1520–1642* (Nottingham: University of Nottingham, 1993)

McRae, A., *How the Scots Won the English Civil War: The Triumph of Fraser's Dragoons* (Stroud: Spellmount, 2011)

Morrill, J., *Revolt in the Provinces: The People of England and the Tragedies of War, 1630–1648* (Harlow: Pearson Education, 1999, first published 1976, 2nd edn)

Morrill, J. (ed.), *The Impact of the English Civil War* (London: Collins & Brown, 1991)

Morrill, J., *The Nature of the English Revolution* (London: Longmans, 1993)

Newman, P. R., *Companion to the English Civil Wars* (Oxford: Facts on File, 1990)

Page, W. (ed.), *Victoria County History of Nottinghamshire*, 2 vols (London: Victoria County History, 1910)

Polkey, A., *The Civil War in the Trent Valley* (Derby: J. H. Hall & Sons, 1992)

Richardson, R. C. (ed.), *The English Civil Wars: Local Aspects* (Stroud: Sutton Publishing, 1997)

Richardson, R. C., *The Debate on the English Revolution* (Manchester: MUP, 1998, 3rd edn)

Roberts, K., *Cromwell's War Machine: The New Model Army, 1645–1660* (Barnsley: Pen and Sword, 2005)

Roots, I., *The Great Rebellion, 1642–1660* (Stroud: Alan Sutton, 1995, 2nd edn)

Scott, M., *Prerogative Court of Canterbury, Wills and other Probate Records,* Public Record Office Readers' Guide, No. 15 (London: PRO, 1997)

Seel, G. E., *The English Wars and Republic, 1637–1660* (London: Routledge, 1999)

Sherwood, R., *The Civil War in the Midlands, 1642–1651* (Stroud: Alan Sutton, 1992)

Smith, N., *Literature and Revolution in England, 1640–1660* (New Haven: Yale University Press, 1994)

Stone, B., *Derbyshire in the Civil War* (Cromford: Scarthin Books, 1992)

Thirsk, Joan, *The Rural Economy of England* (London: The Hambledon Press, 1984)

Thompson, M. W., *The Decline of the Castle* (Cambridge: Cambridge University Press, 2008)

Tincey, J., *Soldiers of the English Civil War (2): Cavalry* (London: Osprey, 1990)

Trotter, E., *Seventeenth Century Life in the Country Parish* (London: Frank Cass & Co., 1919)

Wanklyn, M. and Jones, F., *A Military History of the English Civil War* (Harlow: Pearson Education, 2005)

Wanklyn, M., *Decisive Battles of the English Civil War* (Barnsley: Pen and Sword, 2006)

Ward, A. W. and Waller, A. R. (eds), *Cambridge History of English and American Literature*, 18 vols (Cambridge: Cambridge University Press, 1907–1921)

Wheeler, J. S., *The Irish and British Wars, 1637–1654* (London: Routledge, 2002)

Wilkes, Peter, *The Great Nottingham Goose Fair* (Burton-Upon-Trent: Trent Valley Publications, 1989)

Wood, Alfred C., *Nottinghamshire in the Civil War* (Wakefield: S. R. Reprint, 1971; originally published 1937)

Wood, Alfred C., *A History of Nottinghamshire* (Wakefield: S.R. Reprint, 1971; originally published 1947)

Woolrych, A., *Battles of the English Civil War: Marston Moor, Naseby, Preston* (London: Phoenix Press, 1991)

Wrightson, Keith, *English Society, 1580–1680* (London: Routledge, 1990)

Young, P. (ed.), *Newark upon Trent: The Civil War Siegeworks* (London: HMSO, 1964)

Young, P., and Holmes, R., *The English Civil War: A Military History of the Three Civil Wars, 1642–1651* (London: Eyre Methuen, 1974)

Journal Articles

Barratt, John, 'The Battle of Rowton Heath, 1645', *Journal of the Society for Army Historical Research, 54, 220* (Winter, 1976), pp. 208–224

Beats, L., 'The East Midlands Association, 1642–1644', *Midland History*, 4 (3) (1978), pp. 160–174

Bennett, Martyn, 'The Civil War at Cotes Bridge', *The Leicestershire Historian*, 3 (3), (1984/5), pp. 15–21

Bennett, Martyn, 'Contribution and Assessment: Financial Exactions in the English Civil War, 1642–1646', *War and Society*, 5 (1), (1986), pp. 1–11

Bennett, Martyn, 'The King's Gambit: Charles I and Nottingham in the summer of 1642', *Transactions of the Thoroton Society of Nottinghamshire*, 6 (1992), pp. 133–45

Bennett, Martyn, Jennings, Stuart, Whyld, Martin, 'Two Military Account Books for the Civil War in Nottinghamshire', *Transactions of the Thoroton Society of Nottinghamshire*, 100 (1996), pp. 107–21

Bennett, Martyn., '"My Plundered Townes, my Houses Devastation": The Civil War and North Midlands Life, 1642–1646', *Midland History*, 22:1 (1997), pp. 35–50

Brown, Angela., '"Truth is a Thing Desirable": Propaganda and Nottinghamshire during the English Civil War', *Transactions of the Thoroton Society of Nottinghamshire*, 100 (1996), pp. 95–106

Butler, R. M., 'The Civil War defences at Nottingham', *Transactions of the Thoroton Society of Nottinghamshire*, 53 (1949), pp. 26–33

Edwards, P. R., 'The Supply of Horses to the Parliamentarian and Royalist Armies in the English Civil War', *Historical Research*, 65 (165) (1995), pp. 49–66

Guilford, E. L., 'The surrender of King Charles I to the Scots', *Transactions of the Thoroton Society of Nottinghamshire*, 28 (1924), pp. 81–95

Hill, Christopher, 'Colonel John Hutchinson, 1615–1664: a tercentenary tribute', *Transactions of the Thoroton Society of Nottinghamshire*, 69 (1965), pp. 79–87

Jennings, Stuart B., '"Miserable, Stinking, Infected Town': Pestilence, Plague and Death in a Civil War Garrison, Newark, 1640–1649', *Midland History*, 28 (2003), pp. 51–70

Jennings, Stuart B., 'The Third and Final Siege of Newark (1645–1646) and the Impact of the Scottish Army upon Nottinghamshire and Adjacent Counties', *Midland History*, 37:2 (2012), pp. 142–162

Jennings, Stuart. B., 'Nottinghamshire 1646; Plague, Disruption of Trade and Commerce and the Cancelling of the Goose Fair in the County Town of Nottingham', *Midland History*, 43:2 (2018), pp. 174–189

Kishlansky, Mark A., 'The Army and the Levellers: The Road to Putney', *The Historical Journal*, 22 (4) (December, 1979), pp. 795–824

Race, Sydney, 'The British Museum manuscript of the life of Colonel Hutchinson, and its relation to the published memoirs', *Transactions of the Thoroton Society of Nottinghamshire*, 18 (1914), pp. 35–58

Seddon, P. R., 'Colonel Hutchinson and the disputes between Nottinghamshire Parliamentarians, 1643–1645: New Evidence Analysed', *Transactions of the Thoroton Society of Nottinghamshire*, 98 (1994), pp. 71–81

Wallis, Patrick and Webb, Cliff, 'The Education and Training of Gentry Sons in Early Modern England' *London School of Economics: Economic History Department Working Papers, WP128* (2009)

Wood, Alfred. C., 'A young Nottinghamshire soldier of the Civil War', *Transactions of the Thoroton Society of Nottinghamshire*, 36 (1932), pp. 125–33

Wood, Alfred C., 'Colonel Francis Thornhagh', *Transactions of the Thoroton Society of Nottinghamshire*, 38 (1934), pp. 81–103

Wood, Alfred C., 'A Note on the population of Nottingham in the 17th Century', *Transactions of the Thoroton Society of Nottinghamshire*, 40 (1936), pp. 109–13

Young, Peter, 'The Royalist Army at the Relief of Newark', *Journal of the Society for Army Historical Research,* 30, 124 (Winter, 1952), pp. 145–148